Obsessive-Compulsive Disorder

NEW FINDINGS IN

Obsessive-Compulsive Disorder

Edited by
THOMAS R. INSEL, MD

Staff Psychiatrist,
Clinical Neuropharmacology Branch,
National Institute of Mental Health

AMERICAN PSYCHIATRIC PRESS, INC.
Washington, D.C.

Note: The authors have worked to ensure that all information in this book concerning drug dosages, schedules, and routes of administration is accurate at the time of publication and consistent with standards set by the U.S. Food and Drug Administration and the general medical community. As medical research and practice advance, however, therapeutic standards may change. For this reason and because human and mechanical errors sometimes occur, we recommend that readers follow the advice of a physician directly involved in their care or the care of a member of their family.

This monograph is based on material presented at the 136th Annual Meeting of the American Psychiatric Association. That meeting and this monograph are endeavors to share scientific findings and new ideas. The opinions expressed in this monograph are those of the individual authors and not necessarily those of the American Psychiatric Association.

© 1984 American Psychiatric Association

Library of Congress Cataloging in Publication Data

Main entry under title:

Obsessive-Compulsive Disorder

  (Clinical insights)
  Includes bibliographies.
  1. Obsessive-compulsive neurosis. I. Insel, Thomas R. II. Series. [DNLM: 1. Obsessive—Compulsive disorder. WM 176 N532]
RC533.N48   1984   616.85′227   84-2968
ISBN 0-88048-065-3 (pbk.)

Printed in the U.S.A.

Contents

Contributors

SHERYLE W. ALAGNA, PhD
*Assistant Professor, Medical Psychology,
Uniformed Services University of the Health Sciences*

ROBERT D. COURSEY, PhD
*Associate Professor of Psychology,
University of Maryland*

MARTINE FLAMENT, MD
*Section on Child Psychiatry,
Laboratory of Clinical Science,
National Institute of Mental Health*

EDNA B. FOA, PhD
*Professor, Department of Psychiatry,
Temple University Medical School*

JEAN A. HAMILTON, MD
*Center for the Study of Affective Disorders,
National Institute of Mental Health*

THOMAS R. INSEL, MD
*Staff Psychiatrist,
Clinical Neuropharmacology Branch,
National Institute of Mental Health*

EDWARD A. MUELLER, MD
*Clinical Associate,
Clinical Neuropharmacology Branch,
National Institute of Mental Health*

JOHN C. NEMIAH, MD
*Psychiatrist-in-Chief,
Beth Israel Hospital; and
Professor, Department of Psychiatry,
Harvard Medical School*

Judith L. Rapoport, MD

Chief, Section on Child Psychiatry,
Laboratory of Clinical Science,
National Institute of Mental Health

Gail Steketee, MSW

Department of Psychiatry,
Temple University Medical School

(*Note:* This book was edited by Dr. Insel in his private capacity. No official support or endorsement by the U.S. Public Health Service or by the National Institute of Mental Health is intended or should be inferred.)

Foreword

It is one of the ironies of clinical psychiatry that, although the obsessive-compulsive disorder illuminates the psychoanalytic concept of psychodynamic conflict perhaps better than any other psychoneurosis, its symptoms generally remain impervious to psychoanalytic treatment. To the clinical observer, the patient's struggles with his unacceptable aggressive and scatological impulses, the intense anxiety they arouse in him, and the variety of defenses he employs to control them are all evidence of an intense internal psychic struggle. Unfortunately, such insight, even when it is shared by the patient, seems to have little or no effect on the course of symptoms, and until the advent of newer forms of treatment, patients suffering from obsessive-compulsive disorders were often doomed to a lifetime of painful and debilitating illness.

This book deals with those newer forms of treatment, described within the context of modern psychiatric views of the course, nature, and diagnostic significance of obsessive-compulsive phenomena. Paradoxically, the emergence of more effective therapeutic methods raises questions about the validity of our current diagnostic concepts. Whereas in earlier diagnostic classifications obsessive-compulsive neurosis had been considered a clinical entity separate from phobic and anxiety neurosis, all three are currently viewed in DSM-III as varieties of anxiety disorder. There is some justification for this, since the affect of anxiety is a central feature of each disorder and provides a unifying nucleus for disparate clinical symptoms, which (at least as regards phobic and obsessive-compulsive phenomena) represent different ways of trying to contain and control the anxiety. The remarkable effectiveness of modern behavioral techniques in overcoming many obsessive-compulsive symptoms is based on this centrality of anxiety. Behavior therapy focuses its therapeutic attention on attenuating the anxiety associated with the obsessions and compulsions, and its success in removing the symptoms is logically consistent with the diagnostic concept that obsessive-compulsive neurosis is a form of anxiety disorder.

It comes as rather a surprise, therefore, to discover that antidepressant drugs (both tricyclics and MAO inhibitors) are often dramatically effective against obsessive-compulsive symptoms. As Dr. Insel asks in his chapter on pharmacotherapy, is the obsessive-compulsive disorder perhaps a form of depression? Support for this speculation comes from the dynamic exploration of patients with obsessive-compulsive disorders that often reveals a significant loss associated with depressive affect lying at the core of and behind the surface facade of the presenting obsessive-compulsive symptoms. And clinical experience has long ago indicated that individuals with marked obsessional character traits are often subject to severe mid-life anxious depressions. These observations suggest that obsessive-compulsive phenomena may indeed be related to depressive affect. How, then, are we to square these facts with the concept of obsessive-compulsive neurosis as an *anxiety* disorder? What happens to our diagnostic classifications when the clinical phenomena break through the categorical fences we have erected from our empirical diagnostic criteria? Are there fundamental unifying psychodynamic and pathophysiologic processes underlying mental disorders, the eventual discovery of which will enable clinicians to transcend empirical diagnostic categories and truly to understand the basic mechanisms that produce psychiatric symptoms and determine their relation to one another?

It is one of the virtues of this volume that it does not funk these important questions. Although the authors have been concerned

primarily with describing recent clinical and therapeutic advances, they have appropriately addressed their theoretical implications as well. As a consequence, they have produced a work that
not only is of great practical value to the practicing physician but
also points the way to potential developments in our understanding of mental disorders.

John C. Nemiah, M.D.

1

Obsessive-Compulsive Disorder: The Clinical Picture

Thomas R. Insel, M.D.

1

Obsessive-Compulsive Disorder: The Clinical Picture

Although obsessive-compulsive disorder is a name of recent origin, the syndrome it denotes has been recognized for centuries. Hunter and MacAlpine (1963) have traced the literature on this syndrome back to the 16th century. In English, early terms for obsessive-compulsive disorder were "scruples" and "religious melancholy." French descriptive psychiatrists, following the lead of Esquirol, took an early interest in "folie du doute." By 1878, this interest had spread to Germany. Karl Westphal, who had earlier described agoraphobia, conceptualized a disorder of "Zwangsvorstellungen" (obsessional thoughts). In a talk to the Berlin Medical-Psychological Society, Westphal (1878) elegantly described "ideas that in an otherwise intact intelligence, and without being caused by an emotional or affect-like state, against the will of the person . . . come into the foreground of the consciousness" (p. 735). The terms "obsession" and "compulsion" became associated with this disorder in English psychiatry somewhat later. Obsession, from the Latin verb obsidere, means literally "to besiege"; compulsion comes ultimately from the verb compellere, "to drive together" (Weekley 1967). Both terms suggest what we now recognize as the essence of obsessive-compulsive disorder: the experience of an irrational or reprehensible thought besieging or driving up against the rational or respected self.

In contrast to many other psychiatric syndromes, there has been little added to descriptions of obsessive-compulsive symptoms since the early years of this century. Indeed, those in search of an excellent picture of obsessional phenomena can find the most astute descriptions in Janet's classic, "Les Obsessions et la Psychasthenie" (1903) and in Freud's celebrated "Notes Upon a Case of Obsessional Neurosis" (1909). It is a curious irony that these two brilliant clinicians, after describing the same phenomena, proceed to develop profoundly different theories of causation. Janet formulated obsessional disorder as a deficit in mental energy with a resulting failure of "the will" to control primitive mental functions such as the emotions. Freud, by contrast, stressed the conflict not the deficit. For the obsessional, unconscious impulses clashed with a series of defenses. In place of psychasthenia, Freud invoked regression to the anal-sadistic phase of development as a key to explaining mysterious obsessional phenomena such as undoing, displacement, reaction formation, and even a keen sense of smell.

Although we have "new findings" about obsessive-compulsive disorder, we do not have new comprehensive theories. Janet and Freud used their clinical insights to develop theories of etiology and then suggested therapeutic approaches. Recent investigators have reversed the process. The modern research strategy often begins with a promising new treatment that then suggests a theory of etiology and ultimately alters our perspective on the patients' symptoms. These "new findings" are still in search of "new theories" to explain the intriguing enigma of the obsession.

DEFINITION

Obsessive-compulsive disorder as currently defined in DSM-III differs little from its predecessors, obsessive compulsive reaction of DSM I and obsessive compulsive neurosis of DSM-II (Table 1). Basically an obsession is an intrusive, unwanted mental event usually evoking anxiety or discomfort. A compulsive ritual is a behavior that usually reduces discomfort and yet is experienced with a sense of pressure. The patient attributes both obsessions and

Table 1   DSM-III Criteria for Obsessive-Compulsive Disorder

A1.	*Obsessions:*	Recurrent, persistent ideas, thoughts, images, or impulses that are ego-dystonic, i.e., they are not experienced as voluntarily produced, but rather as thoughts that invade consciousness and are experienced as senseless or repugnant. Attempts are made to ignore or suppress them.
A2.	*Compulsions:*	Repetitive and seemingly purposeful behaviors that are performed according to certain rules or in a stereotyped fashion. The behavior is not an end in itself, but is designed to produce or prevent some future event or situation. However, either the activity is not connected in a realistic way with what it is designed to produce or prevent, or may be clearly excessive. The act is performed with a sense of subjective compulsion (at least initially). The individual generally recognizes the senselessness of the behavior (this may not be true for young children) and does not derive pleasure from carrying out the activity, although it provides a release of tension.
B.		The obsessions or compulsions are a significant source of distress to the individual or interfere with social or role functioning.
C.		Not due to another mental disorder, such as Tourette's Disorder, schizophrenia, major depression, or organic mental disorder.

compulsive rituals to an internal source and both are resisted and lead to interference in functioning.

The problematic concepts here are resistance and interference. Resistance is the struggle against an impulse or intrusive thought. Typically a patient will say "I know my hands aren't contaminated, I know that's an irrational idea, but no matter how much I try, I still have to wash." Resistance, the internal struggle, is not a simple or consistent mental function. Resistance may be high at work but low at home, it may fluctuate day to day, and during episodes when the obsessional symptoms are very severe, it may be absent altogether. Interference is also a dynamic function and, like resistance, it may have a very loose relationship to the severity of symptoms. Many patients deny that their rituals interfere with social role functioning, partly because their rituals have been present for so long that two hours a day in the shower has become "normal." Others manage to function remarkably well in spite of spending three to four hours each day in the bathroom. Interference thus may have more to do with the patient's capacity to adapt to the symptoms rather than reflecting the severity of the symptoms.

Of all the conceivable ways that humans might obsess or

Table 2 Subtypes of the Obsessive-Compulsive Syndrome

Obsession	Compulsion	Resistance	Feature
Contamination	Washing (Restorative)	Moderate	Avoidant Behavior
Doubt	Checking (Preventative)	High	Guilt
Intrusive urges or thoughts	Absent	"Compulsive"	Secretive
Primary obsessional slowness		Low	Low Anxiety

ritualize, patients of diverse backgrounds manifest a fairly re-stricted repertoire of symptoms. Studies from England (Rachman and Hodgson 1980), Hong Kong (Lo 1967), India (Akhtar et al. 1975), Egypt (Okasha et al. 1968), Japan (Inouye 1965), and Norway (Kringlen 1965) describe very similar presentations of the syndrome. There appear to be four major clusters of symptoms (Table 2).

In both English (Rachman and Hodgson 1980) and Indian (Akhtar et al. 1975) samples, approximately 55 percent of obses-sive-compulsive disorder patients describe obsessions about dirt or contamination. Typically, the patient's "fear" may be tinged with disgust and focused on feces, urine, or semen. Rituals of hand washing or showering ensue and the patient may avoid public restrooms, doorknobs, money, or other "contaminated" objects. Some patients may wash their hands 80 or 100 times each day resulting in dermatologic complications. Washing rituals usually but not always lower anxiety (Rachman and Hodgson 1980). In our own series of 13 washers, 10 were more afraid of self-contamination than of contaminating others. Paradoxically many of these patients are quite slovenly (see, for instance, the descrip-tion of Howard Hughes in Barlett and Steele 1979). And they may show resistance that seems half-hearted. For instance, they will describe the obsession as irrational, but when asked to "contami-nate" the therapist or even to touch the floor, they may become quite agitated. When asked more specifically about contamina-tion, most patients reveal only a vague presentiment of dirt or germs or "something bad." Freud (1909, p. 359) at one point observed that "the patients themselves do not know the wording of their own obsessional ideas." He interpreted this as evidence of repression. One might also consider that the rituals may be the primary event for which a vague sense of contamination develops as a secondary explanation.

A second presentation for obsessive-compulsive disorder involves pathologic doubt with compulsive checking. Typically the obsessive-compulsive checker fears the gas jets have been left on or that a bump in the road was a body, doubts which reveal a concern with violence. While uncertainty about carelessness, particularly carelessness that could lead to catastrophic consequences, is common to us all, for the obsessional this uncertainty takes on a gnawing, malignant quality. Checking, which is enough to resolve "normal" uncertainty, often only contributes to the obsessional's doubt. For instance, if after checking, a bump in the road does not appear to be a body, the obsessional then fears that the body may have been knocked into the bushes.

Ultimately, by some inscrutable means, the patient resolves a particular doubt, only to have it replaced by a new obsessional preoccupation. Unlike compulsive washers, these patients may be able to hide their symptoms. Rachman and Hodgson (1980) have described compulsive checking as "preventative" as the fears are often future oriented in contrast to washing, which is "restorative" (p. 116). Resistance, which in this case is the attempt to refrain from checking, contributes to difficulty concentrating and exhaustion from the never-ending assault of nagging uncertainties. Checkers live as if they are the guilty party perpetually in search of a crime. Of 10 such patients in our study, eight described a strict religious upbringing. By contrast, less than 40 percent of patients with other subtypes of obsessive-compulsive disorder gave such a history.

A third clinical picture is that of the pure obsessional. Approximately 25 percent of obsessive-compulsive disorder patients are in this category (Welner et al. 1976; Akhtar et al. 1975). Repetitive, intrusive thoughts, usually sexual or aggressive, and always reprehensible, may be associated with impulses (which have been called horrific temptations) or fearful images. Occasionally the thought may seem relatively neutral to the observer, but for the patient the preoccupation (e.g. "I don't love my wife") invariably seems the worst possible worry. When the obsession is an aggressive impulse, it is most often directed at the one person most valuable to the patient and thus, becomes an indirect attack on the self. When the aggressive impulses are self-directed, they are likely to be bizarre. For instance, a young athlete moving away from home for the first time complained of an obsession to hurl himself down the steps of his new apartment. Only when asked directly did he admit that there were a total of three steps in question. Resistance, which may involve cognitive (e.g., counting or counter-thoughts) rather than behavioral rituals, may take on an obsessional quality. This patient, for instance, resisted the intrusive urge to hurt himself by forcing himself to imagine, in a stereotyped fashion, each possible consequence of giving in to the obsession.

Finally, there is the rare and disabling syndrome of primary obsessional slowness (Rachman 1974). Although slowness results from most rituals, occasionally it becomes the predominant symptom. The patient may take an hour to brush his teeth or two hours to eat breakfast. One such patient presented with stasis pigmentation of both ankles resulting from the eight to 10 hours spent each day at the bathroom sink. Although such patients may have extensive rituals and severe obsessional preoccupations, they manifest very little anxiety. For them, life grinds on at a remarkably low speed.

These four presentations are clusters of symptoms but not discrete syndromes. In many cases washing and checking coexist. In addition, one sees adult patients with pure obsessional complaints who give a history of compulsive handwashing or compulsive checking during young adulthood. Thus, within individuals these different symptom clusters may overlap or may develop sequentially. In our own series of 32 patients who met DSM-III criteria for obsessive-compulsive disorder, nine had pure obsessional symptoms and 23 had rituals. Eight of the nine pure obsessionals had onset during adulthood compared to 11 of the 23 patients with rituals. More washers were female (69 percent) and more checkers were male (70 percent), although in several cases (seven of 23) both washing and checking were present to some degree.

DIFFERENTIAL DIAGNOSIS

Although obsessions and rituals as symptoms are relatively easy to recognize, the syndrome of obsessive-compulsive disorder is less obvious. Obsessions and rituals exist in other psychiatric syndromes and more often than not, patients with primary obsessional disorder will present with features of depression, phobias, or borderline personality disorder. The most common problems in differential diagnosis will be summarized below.

Compulsive Personality

Obsessive-compulsive disorder is not merely a severe form of the compulsive personality. While from a psychodynamic perspective many of the same defenses are present (e.g., isolation of affect, displacement, intellectualization), phenomenologically and epidemologically obsessive-compulsive disorder is qualitatively distinct. Obsessive-compulsive disorder patients have ego-dystonic symptoms, whereas the traits of a patient with a compulsive personality are ego-syntonic, rarely provoke resistance, and are not usually associated with a sense of compulsion. Although many cases of the disorder appear to evolve from a compulsive personality, clearly this is not always the case. In a review of the evidence from seven studies, Black (1974) found between 16 and 36 percent of obsessive-compulsive disorder cases had no history of premorbid obsessional personality traits. Unfortunately, many of these studies were flawed by inconsistent or unclear criteria for obsessional personality. In perhaps the clearest of these papers, Kringlen (1965) reported that 72 percent of 91 obsessional patients had a history of moderate or marked premorbid obsessional traits, especially orderliness. This figure sounds impressive until one sees Kringlen's control data with 53 percent of 91 nonobsessional neurotic patients in the same categories. To the extent that a single personality type is associated with obsessive-compulsive disorder, it might be described more accurately as cautious and introverted (Rachman and Hodgson 1980) rather than fitting the psychoanalytic triad of the obsessional character: orderly, obstinate, and parsimonious. Finally, on the basis of comparative incidence alone, one might presume that when people with compulsive personalities develop severe psychiatric symptoms, they are more likely to present with depression rather than the relatively uncommon syndrome of obsessive-compulsive disorder.

Phobic Disorders

Obsessive-compulsive disorder patients are frequently misla-belled as "germ phobics." Certainly there are major similarities between phobics and compulsive washers. Both have avoidant behavior, both show intense subjective and autonomic responses to focal stimuli, and both respond to similar behavioral interven-tions (Rachman and Hodgson 1980). Many patients with obses-sional traits also have phobias (Videbech 1975), although the extent to which true obsessional disorder and phobia aggregate is not clear. Rosenberg (1967) reported an increased incidence of anxiety neuroses among the relatives of obsessional patients. However, a population study that demonstrated a considerable epidemiologic overlap between other anxiety disorders and pho-bias failed to reveal a single case of obsessional disorder (Weissman et al. 1978).

The distinction between phobias and some less-anxious forms of obsessive-compulsive disorder, such as primary obsessional slowness, is apparent. Among compulsive washers, some (Strauss 1948) have stressed the presence of "disgust" as opposed to fear. A more consistent discriminator is the inescapable nature of the obsession: avoidant behavior can never be entirely successful for the patient with obsessions. Phobias, by contrast, are associated more with external than internal stimuli.

Obsessionals with high levels of anxiety may describe panic-like episodes (see, for instance, Isberg 1981). In contrast to true panic attacks, these episodes are precipitated by a particular obsession. In fact, there is no published evidence that patients with obsessive-compulsive disorder have an increased incidence of panic disorder. Preliminary studies with lactate, a compound that induces panic attacks in predisposed individuals, have found obsessionals nonresponsive (D. Klein, personal communication).

Schizophrenia

Most textbooks state glibly that obsessions can be differentiated from delusions by the presence of insight. An obsession (e.g., of contamination) is ego-dystonic, resisted, and recognized as internal in origin. A delusion (e.g., of being poisoned) is not resisted and believed to be external. Unfortunately, this distinction is not always so easy. As mentioned above, resistance varies with the context. Even the patient who says, "I know my hands are not really contaminated," may act in such a way to reveal a truculent belief to the contrary. Our tradition of labelling this disorder a neurosis has kept us from recognizing that obsessionals who at times become psychotic may still be within the obsessive-compulsive disorder spectrum. The actual transition from obsession to delusion, which occurs in perhaps 12 percent of cases (Gittleson 1966), is not necessarily evidence of "latent" or incipient schizophrenia. In fact, most longitudinal studies of obsessive-compulsive disorder have not documented an increased incidence of schizophrenia (Black 1974), nor is there an increased incidence of schizophrenia in the families of obsessive-compulsive disorder patients (Sakai 1967; Brown 1942). As Sir Aubrey Lewis (1936, p. 330) noted, "The surprising thing is not that some obsessionals become schizophrenic, but that only a few do so. It must be a very short step, one might suppose, from feeling that one must struggle against thoughts that are not one's own, to believing that they are forced upon one by an external agency." That step may episodically be taken, but the transition to a chronic psychotic disorder is unlikely.

Depression

The relationship of obsessional disorder to depression is particularly vexing. Many people develop obsessions when they become depressed, and some evidence suggests that this group of depressives may be unique. Gittleson (1966) in a review of 398 cases of psychotic depression found 31 percent with obsessions.

The presence of obsessions was associated with a higher incidence of premorbid "obsessional personality," "obsessional personality" in the parents, and core depressive symptoms such as diurnal mood variation and depersonalization. Of great interest, depressives with obsessions attempted suicide 6.6 times less frequently than those without obsessions even though the two groups did not differ in hopelessness or "delusion-like" ideas. This apparent "protective" factor from suicide was present even when the obsession involved "killing," but was lost when the obsession became a delusion (when resistance decreased) (Gittleson 1966). Videbech (1975) in a very similar study in Denmark was not able to confirm these "protective" effects on suicide, but corroborated Gittleson's finding that obsessional personality features prior to depression were associated with obsessions during a depressive episode. Videbech (1975) and Vaughan (1976) both found that obsessions were more common in agitated than retarded depressions. In a prospective approach Kendell and Discipio (1970) have administered the Leyton Obsessional Inventory to hospitalized depressed patients and found increases in obessional symptom scores both during the depressive phase and during recovery. By contrast, obsessions appear to be uncommon in mania.

Can these "secondary" obsessions that may be a core symptom of an agitated depression be distinguished from the "primary" obsessions of obsessive-compulsive disorder? Although no formal comparison has been published, the descriptions of obsessional symptoms in primary affective illness suggest that about 50 percent are of aggressive themes in contrast to 19 percent in patients labelled primary obsessionals (Rachman and Hodgson 1980). In addition, the common ruminative symptoms of depression should be distinguished from true obsessions. Ruminations are focused on a past incident, are rarely resisted, and usually take the form of "if only I hadn't. . . . " Obsessions are present or future-oriented, are resisted, and usually are expressed as "I'm afraid I am going to. . . . " However, in many cases, true obsessions emerge as part of a depressive episode, and the distinction between a primary and secondary obsession rests on the order of occurrence. While this distinction may appear arbitrary, there is some evidence that it is useful. In a study of the spectrum of obsessional symptoms, Welner and coworkers (1976) compared the transition from obsessions to depression to the reverse sequence and found the former occurred three times more frequently and was associated with a worse prognosis. Primary obsessional disorder is usually chronic, in contrast to primary depression, which tends to be episodic (Coryell 1981). The disorders also differ in their age of onset (younger for obsessive-compulsive disorder) and male:female ratio (lower for depression).

Other Syndromes

Gilles de la Tourette syndrome is an uncommon disorder characterized by motor and vocal tics often associated with repetitive touching and imitative behavior. Like obsessive-compulsive disorder, Tourette syndrome usually begins in childhood and may involve a struggle with an involuntary act of internal origin. Moreover, true obsessions are common in Tourette's patients (Nee et al. 1980; Cohen et al. 1980), and obsessive-compulsive disorder appears often in their first degree relatives (Montgomery et al. 1982). The distinction arises because obsessive-compulsive disorder patients rarely complain of vocal tics, nor do they present with a movement disorder. Though their compulsive rituals may be performed in a "stereotyped fashion," the cleaning or checking rituals of obsessional patients are considerably more complex and organized than true motor stereotypes.

Anorexia nervosa also shares elements of obsessive-compulsive disorder and may precede or complicate a true obsessional syndrome (Welner et al. 1976). Indeed, in our initial series of 14 obsessional women, three had a history of anorexia nervosa requiring hospitalization during adolescence. Others had obsessions involving food, including a young man with the much resisted obsession, "If I eat, I will die." Obsessive-compulsive disorder patients do not feel they are fat, they do not pursue thinness (although also see Freud 1909, p. 326), and they will force themselves to eat in spite of their fears. Each of our patients with a history of true anorexia nervosa emphasized the difference between "struggling with everyone else then" and "struggling within myself now."

Finally, the post-traumatic stress syndrome may represent a variant of obsessive-compulsive disorder. Both involve intrusive, reprehensible thoughts or images that are resisted and may interfere with functioning. If a distinction can be made, it lies in the documented history of a stress and the fixed content of the intrusive image for patients with a stress response syndrome. In the obsessional, the precipitating event, if present, may appear trivial and the intrusive content frequently shifts to new preoccupations.

PREVALENCE

The actual prevalence of obsessive-compulsive disorder is unknown. The administered prevalence—that is, the number of obsessive-compulsive disorder patients in a treatment population—is probably close to 1 percent with some variance depending on the treatment center (Black 1974). As patients with this disorder are quite secretive, one might expect the actual prevalence to be considerably higher. The current Epidemiologic Catchment Area study sponsored by the National Institute of Mental Health has sought to establish the actual prevalence of several psychiatric disorders by administering the Diagnostic Interview Schedule in a door-to-door survey. Preliminary results (Meyer et al., manuscript submitted for publication) suggest an astonishing rate of 1.3 to 2.0 percent of the general population meeting criteria for obsessive-compulsive disorder. If this diagnostic method is validated and these results are replicated, obsessive-compulsive disorder would appear to be more common in the general population than in the psychiatric clinic. One might then wonder if that tiny fraction of obsessionals who become patients can truly be distinguished by their symptoms, or if some other factor, such as family conflicts, depression, or a particular personality style, might determine which obsessionals become psychiatric patients.

GENETICS

Too few patients with obsessive-compulsive disorder are available to allow for sophisticated adoption studies like those used in research on schizophrenia and affective illness. Studies of the families of obsessional patients have generally yielded a high incidence of obsessional "features" (noninterfering obsessional thoughts or behavior) but not of obsessional disorder per se (Carey and Gottesman 1981; Insel et al. 1983b). There are several reports of monozygotic twins both concordant (Woodruff and Pitts 1964; Marks et al. 1969; McGuffin and Mawson 1980) and discordant (Parker 1964; Hoaken and Schnurr 1980) for obsessive-compulsive disorder. Although the number of reports would suggest that monozygotic twins are more likely to be concordant than discordant, the discrepancy probably reflects less interest in reporting discordant pairs.

Torgersen (1983) reported on nine dizygotic and three monozygotic twins with a proband who met DSM-III criteria for obsessive-compulsive disorder. In this series, none of the pairs were concordant for obsessive-compulsive disorder, although one of the monozygotic and four of the dizygotic co-twins met criteria for some other psychiatric diagnosis. Carey and Gottesman (1981) have also systematically studied a relatively large group of obsessional twins. Of 15 monozygotic twins, five were concordant compared to one of 15 dizygotic twins when the measure of concordance was seeking treatment for obsessional symptoms. Interviews with each of the twin pairs were even more revealing. Obsessional or phobic features were noted in both co-twins for all but two of the monozygotic pairs, whereas less than half of the dizygotic pairs were concordant for this measure. The picture that emerges from these studies is that some predisposition to obsessional behavior is inherited; but, consistent with the preliminary epidemiologic data, the development of a full blown disorder leading to treatment appears to be an uncommon event.

MODELS OF OBSESSIVE-COMPULSIVE BEHAVIOR

One would hope that characterizing the clinical features of a syndrome would lead to a model for research. There are several behavioral (Patel and Malick 1983), electrophysiologic (Redmond 1977), and pharmacologic (Insel et al., in press) models for anxiety; however, relatively little has been developed for obsessive-compulsive behavior. Because obsessions are ultimately cognitive events, the search for an animal model of the disorder has focused on ritualistic or stereotyped behavior. These behaviors may superficially resemble compulsions, but their relationship to other aspects of obsessive-compulsive disorder, such as resistance and interference, remains hypothetical. Nevertheless, the following list of models includes some fascinating leads into future areas of research relevant to the clinical syndrome. For the sake of brevity, these will be mentioned but not discussed in the detail they deserve.

Tinbergen's (1949) original description of displacement activity in male sticklebacks might be viewed as a naturalistic example of compulsive behavior in the face of threat (or conflict). From an evolutionary point of view, stereotypic grooming behavior has been conserved as a displacement activity across a wide range of vertebrate species (Rowell 1961; Mineka et al. 1981), suggesting a considerable adaptive value. Displacement behavior can be elicited by an external threat and may be associated with an internal conflict between impulses for fight or flight. Similarly, in the psychoanalytic formulation, obsessions arise from conflict, as in Freud's famous case (1909, p. 338): "The conflict at the root of his illness was in essentials a struggle between the persisting influence of his father's wishes and his own amatory predilections." From both the ethological and psychoanalytic views, one might argue that compulsive rituals discharge the "anxiety" associated with a conflict. It is still not clear, however, that compulsive washing or checking share the formal characteristics of displacement behavior (Holland 1974), nor is it immediately evident why some individuals in the conflict situation would ritualize, others obsess, and others not manifest anxiety. One intriguing hypothesis from this ethological model is that the compulsive ritual may arise as a primitive "fixed action pattern" for which the obsessions become a secondary explanation.

Laboratory studies of learning behavior may also provide possible models for compulsive behavior. Two classic studies, one with rats (Maier 1949) and one with dogs (Solomon et al. 1953), have demonstrated the onset and persistence of stereotypic behavior associated with certain avoidance paradigms. Like naturalistic displacement behavior, these paradigms are fraught with threat, but in the laboratory these "rituals" may persist even when the overt threat is no longer present (Solomon et al. 1953). This model supports the clinical notion that rituals may become autonomous and it provides an opportunity to test behavioral interventions such as exposure and response prevention (Chapter 3; also see Rush et al. 1983).

Neuroanatomical models have also been suggested, in part, bolstered by the success of psychosurgery for the relief of obsessional symptoms. There is an intriguing literature linking obsessional symptoms in man to the cingulate gyrus (Talairach et al. 1973). Focusing on a related structure, Gray (1982) has recently synthesized a vast array of data that supports the hippocampus as a "comparator" of expected and perceived events. When this comparator malfunctions, compulsive checking results. Along these lines, Devenport (1979) has observed "superstitious" behavior in rats with hippocampal lesions. However, if the hippocampus were dysfunctional in obsessive-compulsive disorder, one would expect some memory deficit which has not been consistently demonstrated (see Chapter 2).

As stereotypes frequently develop with stimulant abuse, one might assume that amphetamine toxicity would model features of obsessive-compulsive disorder. Actually acute amphetamine administration decreases rather than increases the symptoms of obsessive-compulsive disorder patients (Insel et al. 1983a). This paradox may reflect a difference between acute and chronic drug administration. It is also important to distinguish obsessions that are complex mental events and stereotypies that are automatic motor acts. Recent results with the opiate antagonist naloxone suggest an alternative pharmacologic model of obsessional doubt (Insel and Pickar 1983).

Finally, it needs to be stated that obsessions and compulsions develop normally in childhood and that intrusive thoughts and repetitive, senseless behaviors can be elicited from most normal adults, particularly in response to threat or risk. Indeed, one can imagine a normal analogue for each of the subtypes of the disorder. For instance, the sense of contamination and the urge to wash repetitively is often noted by people working with radioactivity (an invisible, odorless "threat") for the first time. Following an auto accident involving a pedestrian, drivers frequently become more cautious and may check their paths repeatedly. The urge to shout an obscenity during a religious service is a common and "normal" example of an intrusive, repugnant thought. These examples may be useful for revealing certain aspects of the patients' experience, but they are not models of obsessional disorder. An external, precipitating event, such as radiation or an auto accident, is generally not present for obsessional patients. Furthermore, although there is considerable individual variation in the rate of habituation, normal urges to wash, check, or shout attenuate with time. Perhaps the major difference between these normal phenomena and the symptoms of obsessive-compulsive disorder resides in the poorly understood domains of resistance and interference. Anyone seeking to understand this clinical syndrome fully must ultimately explain how a thought or impulse that for others is a passing whim, becomes, for the obsessional, a source of unremitting anguish and disability.

CONCLUSION

Obsessive-compulsive disorder is a syndrome that is heterogeneous, including subtypes that overlap with both anxiety and affective disorders. The syndrome may be far more common than currently realized and may, from a biological point of view, be continuous with "normal" responses to threat. Normal obsessions might be conceptualized as adaptive responses to threat that quickly habituate. By contrast, for obsessive-compulsive disorder patients, the original threat may not be apparent, there is a failure of habituation, and over a course of several months the obsession that has become autonomous may evolve into a threat of its own.

References

Akhtar S, Wig NH, Verma VK, et al: A phenomenological analysis of symptoms in obsessive compulsive neuroses. Br J Psychiatry 127:342–348, 1975

American Psychiatric Association: Diagnostic and Statistical Manual of Mental Disorders, 3rd ed. Washington, DC, American Psychiatric Association, 1980

Barlett DL, Steele JB: Empire: The Life, Legend, and Madness of Howard Hughes. New York, WW Norton & Co, 1979, pp 232–235

Black A: The natural history of obsessional neurosis, in Obsessional States. Edited by Beech HR. London, Methuen & Co, 1974

Brown F: Heredity in the psychoneuroses. Proceedings of the Royal Society of Medicine 35:785–790, 1942

Carey G, Gottesman II: Twin and family studies of anxiety, phobic, and obsessive disorders, in Anxiety: New Research and Changing Concepts. Edited by Klein DF, Rabkin J. New York, Raven Press, 1981

Cohen DJ, Detlor J, Young J, et al: Clonidine ameliorates Gilles de la Tourette syndrome. Arch Gen Psychiatry 37:1350–1357, 1980

Coryell W: Obsessive compulsive disorder and primary unipolar depression. J Nerv Ment Dis 169:220–224, 1981

Devenport LD: Superstitious bar pressing in hippocampal and septal rats. Science 205:721–722, 1979

Freud S (1909): Notes upon a case of obsessional neurosis, in Collected Papers, vol. 3. New York, Basic Books, 1959, pp 293–383

Gittleson N: The fate of obsession in depressive psychosis. Br J Psychiatry 112:705–708, 1966

Gray JA: The Neuropsychology of Anxiety. New York, Oxford University Press, 1982

Hoaken PCS, Schnurr R: Genetic factors in obsessive-compulsive neurosis? Can J Psychiatry 25:167–172, 1980

Holland HC: Displacement activity as a form of abnormal behavior in animals, in Obsessional States. Edited by Beech HR. London, Methuen & Co, 1974, pp 161–174

Hunter R, MacAlpine I: Three Hundred Years of Psychiatry. London, Oxford University Press, 1963

Inouye E: Similar and dissimilar manifestations of obsessive-compulsive neurosis in monozygotic twins. Am J Psychiatry 121:1171–1175, 1965

Insel TR, Pickar D: Naloxone administration in obsessive compulsive disorder: a report of two cases. Am J Psychiatry 140:1219–1220, 1983

Insel TR, Hamilton J, Guttmacher L, et al: d-Amphetamine in obsessive compulsive disorder. Psychopharmacology 80:231–235, 1983a

Insel TR, Hoover C, Murphy DL: Parents of patients with obsessive compulsive disorder. Psychol Med 13:807–811, 1983b

Insel TR, Ninan PT, Aloi J, et al: A benzodiazepine receptor mediated model of anxiety. Arch Gen Psychiatry (in press)

Isberg R: A comparison of phenelzine and imipramine in an obsessive-compulsive patient. Am J Psychiatry 138:1250–1251, 1981

Janet P: Les Obsessions et la Psychasthenie. Paris, Bailliere, 1903

Kendell RE, Discipio WJ: Obsessional symptoms and obsessional personality traits in patients with depressive illnesses. Psychol Med 1:65–72, 1970

Kringlen E: Obsessional neurotics: a long term follow-up. Br J Psychiatry 111:709–722, 1965

Lewis AJ: Problems of obsessional illness. Proceedings of the Royal Society of Medicine 29:325–336, 1936

Lo W: A follow-up study of obsessional neurotics in Hong Kong Chinese. Br J Psychiatry 113:823–832, 1967

Maier NRF: Frustration: The Study of Behavior Without a Goal. New York, McGraw-Hill, 1949

Marks IM, Crowe M, Drewe E, et al: Obsessive-compulsive neurosis in identical twins. Br J Psychiatry 115:991–998, 1969

McGuffin P, Mawson D: Obsessive compulsive neurosis: two concordant twin pairs. Br J Psychiatry 137:285–287, 1980

Mineka S, Suomi SJ, Delizio R: Multiple peer separations in adolescent monkeys: an opponent process interpretation. J Exp Psychol [Gen] 110:56–85, 1981

Montgomery MA, Clayton PJ, Friedhoff AJ: Psychiatric illness in Tourette Syndrome patients and first degree relatives, in Gilles de la Tourette Syndrome. Edited by Friedhoff AJ, Chase TN. New York, Raven Press, 1982, pp 335–339

Myers JK, Weissman MM, Tischler GL, et al: The prevalence of psychiatric disorders in three communities: 1980-1982, Manuscript submitted for publication

Nee LE, Caine ED, Polinsky RJ: Gilles de la Tourette Syndrome: clinical and family study of 50 cases. Ann Neurol 7:41–49 1980

Okasha A, Kamel M, Hassan A: Preliminary psychiatric observations in Egypt. Br J Psychiatry 114:949–956, 1968

Parker N: Close identification in twins discordant for obsessional neurosis. Br J Psychiatry 110:496–504, 1964

Patel JB, Malick JB: Neuropharmacological profile of an anxiolytic, in Anxiolytics: Neurochemical, Behavioral, and Clinical Perspectives. Edited by Malick JB, Enna SJ, Yamamura H. New York, Raven Press, 1983, pp 173–188

Rachman SJ: Primary obsessional slowness. Behav Res Ther 111:463–471, 1974

Rachman SJ, Hodgson RJ: Obsessions and Compulsions. Englewood Cliffs, NJ, Prentice Hall, 1980

Redmond DE: Alterations in the function of the nucleus locus coeruleus: a possible model for studies of anxiety, in Animal Models in Psychiatry and Neurology. Edited by Hanin I, Usdin E. New York, Pergamon Press, 1977, pp 293–306

Rosenberg C: Family aspects of obsessional neurosis. Br J Psychiatry 113:405–413, 1967

Rowell CHF: Displacement grooming in the chaffinch. Animal Behavior 9:38–63, 1961

Rush DK, Mineka S, Suomi SJ: Therapy for helpless monkeys. Behav Res Ther 21:297–301, 1983

Sakai T: Clinico-genetic study on obsessive compulsive neurosis. Bull Osaka Med Sch [Suppl] 12:323–331, 1967

Solomon RL, Kamin LJ, Wynne LC: Traumatic avoidance learning: the outcomes of several extinction procedures with dogs. Journal of Abnormal Social Psychology 48:291–299, 1953

Straus E: On obsession: a clinical and methodological study. New York, Coolidge Foundation, 1948

Talairach J, Bancand J, Geier S, et al: The cingulate gyrus and human behavior. Electroencephalogr Clin Neurophysiol 34:45–52, 1973

Tinbergen N: The Social Behavior of Animals. London, Methuen & Co, 1949

Torgersen S: Genetic factors in anxiety disorders. Arch Gen Psychiatry 40:1085–1089, 1983

Vaughan M: The relationship between obsessional personality, obsession in depression and symptoms of depression. Br J Psychiatry 129:36–39, 1976

Videbech T: The psychopathology of anancastic endogenous depression. Acta Psychiatr Scand 52:336–373, 1975

Weekley E: An Etymological Dictionary of Modern English. New York, Dover, 1967

Weissman MM, Myers JK, Harding PS: Psychiatric disorders in a U.S. urban community. Am J Psychiatry 135:459–462, 1978

Welner A, Reich T, Robins E, et al: Obsessive compulsive neurosis: record, family, and follow-up studies. Compr Psychiatry 17:527–539, 1976

Westphal K: Ueber Zwangsvorstellungen. Archiv für Psychiatrie und Nervenkrankheiten 8:734–750, 1878

Woodruff R, Pitts FN: Monozygotic twins with obsessional neurosis. Am J Psychiatry 120:1075–1080, 1964

2

Childhood Obsessive-Compulsive Disorder

Martine Flament, M.D.
Judith L. Rapoport, M.D.

2

Childhood Obsessive-Compulsive Disorder

Childhood obsessive-compulsive disorder, unlike many other childhood disorders, presents in a form virtually identical to the full adult syndrome. The same diagnostic criteria apply to both children and adults, the clinical phenomenology is strikingly similar, and the disorder when it arises early in life is remarkably continuous from childhood to adulthood. Therefore, research on children with this disorder is of particular interest in understanding the nature of this severe and disabling illness whose natural course often runs over a lifetime.

INCIDENCE

The earliest descriptions of obsessive-compulsive neurosis in children date back to the beginning of this century. Janet, in 1903, reported a case in a five-year-old child. Freud's (1955) famous patient, the Rat Man, had his first symptoms around age six or seven. Other authors, like Barton Hall in 1935 and Kanner in 1957, described "obsessional states" in children that began as early as age four. Berman (1942), who found six cases of obsessive-compulsive neurosis out of 2,800 admissions to the children's ward at New York's Bellevue Hospital, noted that the three most severely afflicted patients had "neurotic disturbances" from early childhood.

24

The first systematic descriptions of obsessions in children came from retrospective histories obtained from adult obsessional patients. Onset of obsessional illness between age four and 10 was reported by Pollitt (1957) in 22 percent of his adult patients and by Warren (1960) in 60 percent of his smaller sample. Ingram (1961), Kringlen (1965), and Lo (1967) consistently reported childhood symptoms in 20 to 36 percent of obsessional adult neurotics. Black (1974) in his cumulative review of these and other studies suggested that nearly one-third of 357 adult cases had onset between ages five and 15.

To date there have been few specific studies of childhood obsessive-compulsive disorder. In 1965, Judd's retrospective chart examination of 405 children seen at UCLA Neuropsychiatric Institute yielded five cases meeting strict diagnostic criteria for obsessive-compulsive neurosis, which made up 1.2 percent of the children's psychiatric cases. More recently in the same center, Hollingsworth et al. (1980) found only 17 cases in a retrospective examination of more than 8,000 inpatient and outpatient clinical records, an incidence of 0.2 percent of the child psychiatric cases. The first prospective study might have been that of Adams (1973), who reviews his experience with 49 children diagnosed as obsessive-compulsive (33), mixed neurosis (6), or obsessive character (10). However, Adams did not demarcate state and trait for particular measures, nor did he use standardized methods for distinguishing between diagnoses.

Because of the rarity of obsessive-compulsive disorder in childhood, systematic study from epidemiologic surveys of even large populations is not possible. The famous Isle of Wight study in England (Rutter et al. 1970) that looked at more than 2,000 10- and 11-year-olds, for example, did not find a single case.

NATIONAL INSTITUTE OF MENTAL HEALTH STUDY

A study of childhood obsessive-compulsive disorder, therefore, must be done through a case-finding approach. This was started in 1977 at the National Institute of Mental Health (NIMH). National and local publications carried notices about our search for children and adolescents aged six to 18 years with primary obsessive-compulsive disorder. Referrals came from psychiatrists or primary care physicians and were screened for inclusion in a systematic prospective study involving clinical, family, and neurobiological measures as well as a psychopharmacological trial.

Inclusion criteria were those of DSM-III, namely rituals and/or repetitive thoughts resisted by the patient and causing significant interference in home, school, or interpersonal functioning. In addition, symptoms had to be present for at least one year and constitute a primary and "pure" syndrome: applicants were rejected if there was any evidence of thought disorder (18 cases) or delusional system (five cases), mental retardation or other neurological damage (four cases), or of primary depressive illness (three cases). Other reasons for exclusion were either symptoms too mild at time of evaluation (six cases) or uncooperativeness with study procedures (five cases). Twenty-seven children with primary obsessive-compulsive disorder have now completed the baseline study and 19 of them have completed the pharmacological trial. They were matched with controls for age, sex, IQ, and handedness for comparison on neuropsychological and psycholinguistic tests. Control computerized axial tomography (CT) scans were obtained from a primary care hospital for comparison with the patients' scans.

Clinical Features

In our sample of 27 subjects, boys predominate (2:1), which follows the trend of 3:1 reported both by Hollingsworth et al. (1980) and Adams (1973). The mean age at admission was 14.4 years, with a range from 10 to 18 years. As has been reported with adult patients, several years had often elapsed between onset of illness and beginning of treatment. Unlike depression and schizophrenia where there is a peak of onset in adolescence, many of these children became sick during prepubertal years (see Table 1). The mean age of onset was 10.25 years, and average duration of the illness had been four years.

Onset was acute for some subjects but gradual in the majority. With few exceptions, family and patient reports of precipitating

Table 1 Age of Onset and Symptoms in 27 Obsessive-Compulsive Children

Age of Onset (years)	Cases	(%)
2 - 4	3	(11)
7 - 9	7	(26)
10 - 14	15	(56)
15 - 16	2	(7)
Primary Presenting Symptoms		
Washing germs, sperm, sticky substances	14	
Touching, body movements	3	
Preoccupation with sharp objects, death	1	
"Straightening room," checking	3	
Repetitive thoughts	5	
Repeating sentences	1	

events were unconvincing. Events were of uncertain significance to the patient, careful questioning did not show agreement within the family about the actual relationship of onset of the disorder to the presumed precipitating event, and the severity of illness seemed out of proportion to the "precipitating event" or to the familial disturbance. This contrasts with Judd's observation that onset was often sudden and linked with a symbolically significant precipitating event and Hollingsworth's finding that in 15 of 17 cases, obsessive thoughts appeared clearly related to frightening situations at home.

On psychological testing, the group scored in the average intelligence range: on the Wechsler Intelligence Scale for Children (Revised), the mean $\pm$ SD full scale IQ was 105.9 $\pm$ 12.9; verbal IQ, 105.8 $\pm$ 11.8; and performance IQ, 104.7 $\pm$ 13.9. This is of interest because it was previously thought that these children had superior intelligence. Intelligence and Bender-Gestalt tests gave no evidence of organicity for the group as a whole, although about 25 percent of the subjects showed significant subtest scatter (Behar et al. in press). Peabody Individual Achievement scores showed that the group achieved at grade level (when not acutely ill) and, in line with other studies, neither major depression nor psychosis was prominent on projective testing.

There was a variety of premorbid personality functioning, supporting a rather remarkable discontinuity between disorder and trait. Very few children were described as having always been meticulous in their habits, overly concerned with cleanliness, or overly ruminative. Furthermore, while hospitalized, almost none of the patients appeared orderly or clean in matters unrelated to their rituals. The premorbid pattern of the group, with few exceptions, had not been markedly deviant. Most children (15 cases) tended to be good, although not outstanding, students, and to have shy and nonaggressive personalities. Nevertheless, a picture of these children as "marked introverts" would be inaccurate; only nine were described as isolated and somewhat withdrawn. Some parents recalled a moderate amount of stubborn and argumentative behavior, and in six cases behavior problems or antisocial traits had been noted. Symptoms produced strong family conflicts, but this was most often a clear change from previous functioning. Lewis (1936) observed a predominance of two types of personalities among those obsessive individuals whose symptoms dated back to childhood, the one "obstinate, morose, and irritable," the other "vacillating, unsure of himself, submissive." Some of the children in our group resembled the second type. There was no evidence for "high neuroticism" or increased previous psychopathology as has been described retrospectively in adult patients (Rosenberg 1967; Slade 1974; Kringlen 1965).

The primary presenting symptoms are summarized in Table 1. Similar to adults, obsessional children usually present with combined obsessive thoughts and compulsive rituals. The most frequent picture is fear of contamination, with the associated rituals of washing, cleaning, and avoiding touching. Other common rituals include checking, arranging, straightening, gesturing, pacing; complex motor rituals can affect even walking. Compulsions typically focus on warding off some dreaded event, usually harm coming to self or family members, or forbidden sexual or religious words and ideas. Obsessive thoughts occasionally concern "meaningless" material (counting, repeating words or sentences) and may occur in the absence of rituals, but, more often they present as very crude fantasies that have to be fought through cognitive or behavioral rituals.

Obsessive-compulsive children present symptoms and a degree

Table 2 Psychiatric Diagnoses in 54 Parents of 27 Obsessive-Compulsive
            Children

Diagnosis	Mothers	Fathers*	Total	(%)
None	18	15	33	(61)
Alcoholism	2	4	6	(11)
Depressive Personality	1	1	2	(4)
Minor Dysphoria	4	1	5	(9)
Generalized Anxiety	0	1	1	(2)
Personality Disorder (unspecified)	0	3	3	(5)
Affective Disorder	1	1	2	(4)
Schizophrenia	1	1	2	(4)
Total	27	27	54	

Note. Two children adopted.
*Information was obtained from the mother in three cases.

of incapacitation comparable to those of afflicted adults. The most
striking feature is the severity of the psychopathology in the
absence of formal thought disorder. Mental status is relatively
intact and these children's relatedness and sensible discussion of
their problems is in almost eerie contrast with their incapacity.
The notion of insight bears some peculiarities in children: although on reflection they universally acknowledge that their
worries and habits are senseless, in stressful situations insight and
resistance fluctuate.

In spite of the severity of the disorder and resulting constriction
of functioning, only three of the children in the NIMH study met
criteria for major depressive disorder at the time of entry into the
study. The depressive symptoms of these patients clearly occurred
one or two years after the obsessive rituals had begun. However, all
of the patients had had, at some point of their illness, symptoms of
depression, sometimes sleep disturbances, weight loss, and
thoughts of killing themselves because of their obsessive disorder.
Most of them would have met DSM-III criteria for major depressive disorder at some time during their obsessional illness.

Family Psychopathology

Studies with children provide an opportunity to assess family
functioning and psychopathology of family members with comparative ease. In the NIMH study, all first-degree relatives were

evaluated: family members older than 17 were interviewed using the SADS-L (Schedule for Affective Disorders and Schizophrenia-lifetime version), minor siblings were given the Diagnostic Interview for Children and Adolescents (DICA) of Herjarnic and Campbell (1977). Diagnoses were made according to DSM-III criteria.

Unlike the parental psychopathology found in other studies (Lewis 1936; Brown 1942), in our sample, the parent's psychiatric disorders were not striking and were nonspecific (see Table 2). As in Insel's study (Insel et al., 1983), no parent had obsessive-compulsive disorder and 61 percent had no lifetime diagnosis at all. None of the parents reported being meticulous to a degree that it would interfere with their life or work. Parental attitudes did not appear particularly perfectionistic as reported by Kanner (1957), nor did we have evidence for unusually strict upbringing in the families of our patients, although this has been described in other studies (Adams 1973; Kringlen 1965).

In the sibling evaluation (Table 3), the younger group was characterized by a relatively high frequency of impulse control disorders (hyperactivity, conduct disorder) and learning disability but a notable absence of anxiety or obsessive-compulsive syndromes. In the group of siblings age 18 or older, there were two cases of obsessive-compulsive disorder and a few with anxiety disorders but no cases of major depression or schizophrenia. All the obsessive-compulsive and anxiety disorder cases were limited to a single family of 10 children.

Thus, with this one exception, the family psychopathology in our sample indicated some nonspecific disturbances but did not support the idea that this is typically a genetically based illness. Our patients' families had little psychopathology or medical illness compared with those in Hollingsworth et al.'s study in which 82 percent of the parents had severe psychiatric and/or medical illness, 20 percent had obsessive-compulsive neurosis, and 23 percent of the probands also suffered from serious medical illness. Lewis (1936) in a study of 206 siblings of adult patients reported some psychiatric disorder in 45 percent and pronounced obsessional traits in 21 percent. Rosenberg (1967) found that 9

Table 3 Psychiatric Diagnoses in 58 Siblings of 27 Obsessive-Compulsive Children

Age Group (N), Diagnosis	No. with diagnosis	(%)
≥ 18 Years Old (32)		
No Diagnosis	18	(56)
Depressive Personality	3	(9)
Generalized Anxiety	3	(9)
Panic Disorder	2	(6)
Alcoholism	3	(9)
Phobic Reaction	1	(3)
Drug Abuse	1	(3)
Obsessive Compulsive Disorder	2	(6)
< 18 Years Old (26)		
No Diagnosis	16	(62)
Depressive Personality	2	(8)
Attention Deficit Disorder	3	(11)
Learning Disability	2	(8)
Organic Brain Syndrome	1	(4)
Unsocialized Aggressive Conduct Disorder	3	(11)
Anorexia Nervosa	1	(4)

Note. Multiple diagnoses were used.

percent of the first degree relatives of 144 adult patients had received psychiatric treatment but obsessional disorder was diagnosed in only two cases (an incidence of 0.4 percent). The presence of anorexia nervosa in one of our siblings is of interest; Welner and associates (1976) found concurrent anorexia in five of 150 adult obsessive patients. None of our patients themselves had a history of earlier hyperactivity, although such an association has been reported (Jessner 1963).

IS THERE A NEUROPSYCHOLOGICAL DEFICIT?

Since the first modern descriptions of the syndrome, obsessive-compulsive disorder has been widely viewed as psychological in genesis. However, it is notoriously intractable to psychotherapeutic intervention and evidence implicating altered neurological function has been accumulating along several lines of inquiry, as reviewed elsewhere (Elkins et al. 1980).

History of Birth Trauma

Capstick and Seldrup (1977) found a history of abnormal birth events in 11 of 33 unselected obsessionals, compared to a control group of patients with other psychiatric disorders in which birth complications occurred only twice. Certain differences in presentation of obsessional symptoms ("bizarre rituals") distinguished patients with abnormal birth history from those without it. In the NIMH sample, pre- and perinatal problems were reported for five (20 percent) of the nonadopted children.

Electroencephalography

Various incidences of EEG abnormalities in adult obsessive-compulsives have been reported by several authors. One should keep in mind, however, that most of the studies are old and the diagnostic criteria were not rigorously defined. Patients with obsessional symptoms associated with other serious forms of psychopathology were sometimes included along with those with pure obsessive-compulsive disorder. Furthermore, the criteria for EEG evaluation were not standardized. Pacella et al. (1944) in a study of 31 patients presenting "obsessive compulsive phenomena" as a dominant clinical feature, found 64 percent with EEG abnormalities, most often serial slow wave activity at rest or after hyperventilation. This report was not confirmed by Rockwell and Simons (1947) who observed abnormal EEGs in only two of 11 cases with simple obsessive compulsive neurosis, or by Ingram and McAdam (1960) who registered overt EEG abnormalities in only one of 22 cases of "typical obsessive compulsive neurosis." In a study of 110 obsessive compulsive patients, Inouye (1973) reported a 48 percent incidence of nonspecific EEG abnormalities, such as slowing, dysrhythmia, and provocation of slow activities with hyperventilation. Similarly in 1974, Sugiyama found abnormal EEGs in 49 percent of 73 obsessive compulsive neurotics; abnormal records consisted of eight cases of non-paroxysmal and 28 of paroxysmal EEGs with 10 showing seizure patterns.

In contrast, Insel et al. (1983) found abnormal EEGs in only two (11 percent) of 18 DSM-III diagnosed adult obsessive compulsive disorder patients. In our cohort, four EEGs (15 percent) were read as (mildly) abnormal: two had a mild excess of bilateral nonspecific theta activity, either diffuse or centrally predominant; one showed intermittent mixed bioccipital slow wave activity; and the last one transient bilateral slow waves, predominantly in the frontal region. In addition, six EEGs were labeled as normal but contained intermittent slow activity usually in the 4–6 Hz range not sufficient to be considered abnormal. Thus, in our experience, EEG abnormalities in children with obsessive-compulsive disorder appear uncommon, mild, and nonspecific.

Neuropsychological Testing

Seventeen obsessive-compulsive children from the NIMH sample were compared to controls on a battery of neuropsychological tests. The details of this study have been described elsewhere (Behar et al. in press). In brief, measures of memory and attention include the Rey Word List Learning (immediate free recall of a standard list of 15 words), a simple Reaction Time task, and a Two-Flash Threshold procedure (subject's ability to discriminate between single and double flashes). Perception and spatial judgment are tested with Money's Road Map Test of Directional Sense in which the subject is presented a simulated street map of a city and asked to imagine traveling along a route indicated by a dotted line; at each intersection he must indicate whether he would turn right or left, half of the route is designated to move away from him, the other half moving toward the subject who has to reverse his own left-right reference. Patients with frontal lobe lesions have been reported to do poorly on this task. Perceptual-motor integration and memory are evaluated on the Rey-Osterrieth Complex Figure Test (copy and memory), and the Stylus Maze Learning. In the latter, the subject learns by trial and error an unknown pathway connecting the start and goal points on a 10×10 grid of terminals placed on a board. Performance on the Stylus Maze has been reported to be sensitive to right frontal and temporal lobe disorders.

There were no significant differences between obsessional subjects and controls on measures of attention, memory, or decision time. However, patients made significantly more errors on the Road Map Test ($p = .01$), revealing a relative inability to make spatial and directional judgments using their own body as a reference. In addition, obsessionals were significantly different from controls on the Stylus Maze Learning ($p = .0004$), making more errors across trials and breaking the rules more often, indicating a relative inability to discern unstated patterns. On the Rey-Osterrieth Complex Figure copy, the difference between the performance scores of the two groups did not reach significance, although patients took significantly longer ($p = .02$) to copy the figure and their strategies for completing the task lacked the refinement seen in normal controls.

What is remarkable is the relative specificity of these deficits, in the absence of evidence for general impairment, poor attention, or disturbed memory. In addition, these findings cannot be explained by obsessional slowness since reaction times, two-flash thresholds, and decision times for the patients were the same as those of controls. Similar patterns of spatial-perceptual deficits on both Stylus Maze Learning and the Road Map Test have been reported in subjects with confirmed frontal lobe damage (Fedio et al. 1979).

Clearly, a deficit shared by patients with focal brain lesions does not necessarily implicate localized neuropathology. Nevertheless, some "frontal" neuropsychological deficits have emerged from other studies of obsessional patients. Flor-Henry and coworkers (1979) conducted a controlled neuropsychological investigation on 11 consecutive adult patients with primary obsessive-compulsive syndrome. Both electroencephalographic and individual test results were interpreted as indicating bilateral frontal dysfunction, with more left hemisphere pathology. In addition, on the Wechsler Adult Intelligence Scale (WAIS), patients were significantly impaired on the digit span and digit symbol subtests, again consistent with frontal lobe dysfunction. Insel and associates (1983) could not replicate Flor-Henry's findings: their 18 adult obsessionals scored within the normal range on the Halstead-Reitan Battery (HRB). However, four subjects had average impairment ratings on the HRB high enough to suggest organic deficits, and more than half of the patients were impaired on the tactile performance test, suggesting a possible deficit in spatial judgment.

Psycholinguistic Testing

If obsessional children had left frontal lobe dysfunction, one might expect to find problems with language. To investigate this possibility, we administered selected subtests from the Neurosensory Center Comprehensive Examination for Aphasia to a subsample of patients and controls (Rapoport et al. 1981). These are sensitive measurements of specific language impairment that do not depend on memory, learning skills, or visual decoding. In addition, subjects were tested on a Dichotic Listening Task which consists of pairs of phonetic consonant-vowel nonsense syllables sent simultaneously to both ears. In normal adults, the perception of such syllables is known to rely more on the processing mechanisms located in the dominant speech hemisphere than on those in the right hemisphere. The laterality index (right ear advantage divided by total percent of correct reporting) is a stable measure of right ear advantage independent of performance level for each subject.

Preliminary data analysis from the first nine subjects (Rapoport et al. 1981) showed that patients did not differ from normal controls on language expression and comprehension tests. For dichotic listening however, the laterality indices were lower in the obsessional group ($p < .01$). Raw scores indicated that the mean total percent of correct reporting was equal in the two groups. Thus, the patients' lack of laterality is not due to deficient speech perception, but rather to less dominance of the left hemisphere during competitive processing.

Handedness is related to language laterality. In our study, 22 percent of our patients were left-handed, which is higher than the percentage (10 percent) in the general population and approaches 27 percent as reported by Flor-Henry and associates (1979).

Previous reports of no predominance of left hemisphere EEG activity during verbal task performance, coupled with the high rate of left-handedness and the dichotic listening results, suggest a reduced left hemisphere dominance in obsessive patients. Yet, such findings might not be specific, because lack of laterality has been reported for other psychiatric conditions, including depression (Wexler 1980).

Computerized Axial Tomography

Ventricular brain ratio (VBR) measures were obtained from brain CT scans of 17 of the NIMH obsessive-compulsive children and matched controls (Behar et al, 1984). As a group, the patients had a significantly higher mean VBR (percent) than the control group (mean ± SD, 4.5 ± 3.3 vs. 2.4 ± 1.7; $p < .03$). Among patients, 25 percent had VBR's greater than 2 standard deviations above the control mean, although most were within normal limits. Ventricular size did not correlate with sex, index or onset age, severity or duration of illness, previous drug treatment, EEG abnormalities, history of birth trauma, or neuropsychological test scores.

Ventricular enlargement has been documented in a substantial proportion of psychiatric patients, both children (Caparulo et al. 1981; Campbell et al. 1982) and adults (Weinberger et al. 1979; Pearlson et al. 1981). However, this finding does not appear specific to any particular disorder or symptom and little is known still about its significance. Our findings with obsessional children seem to be the first report of CT scan abnormalities for patients with an anxiety disorder. They are not consistent with those of Insel and associates (1983) who did not find cerebral CT scans of 10 adult obsessional patients to be different from a matched group of nonpsychiatric control subjects for VBR, asymmetry and sulcal prominence measures. None of the 10 obsessional subjects, including two with abnormal EEGs and four with high average impairment ratings on the HRB, had a VBR greater than two standard deviations above the control mean. The discrepancy between our results and those of Insel et al. might point to a developmental abnormality apparent in children that is no longer present in adults with obsessive-compulsive disorder.

TREATMENT

In 1935, Barton Hall wrote very enthusiastic reports of the psychological treatment of children with obsessive-compulsive neurosis. Somewhat later, successful psychoanalyses were reported (Bornstein 1949; Chetnik 1969). Nevertheless, obsessive-compulsive disorder in children, as in adults, generally resists psychodynamic treatment (Black 1974). A few cases of successful outcome with strategic, problem-focusing psychotherapy have been reported (Weiner 1967; O'Connor 1983). Family therapy has been used with benefits in some instances (Fine 1973; Hafner et al. 1981).

Individual reports indicate that behavioral techniques similar to those used in adults also apply in children. For example, Bolton et al. (1983) successfully treated 15 cases of adolescent obsessionals with response prevention and family sessions. Medications (diazepam, clomipramine) were used together with other treatment modalities in rare instances. Otherwise, to our knowledge, no study or even case report of drug treatment for childhood obsessive-compulsive disorder has been published, except for our preliminary report of nine children treated with clomipramine, desmethylimipramine, and placebo (Rapoport et al. 1980).

The present study included a placebo controlled trial of clomipramine for 19 subjects. After a two-week washout period and a one-week baseline evaluation, there were two five-week consecutive phases of placebo or clomipramine. Medication was administered in double-blind fashion with randomized order for the two treatments. Active drug was given in divided doses of 50 mg with a maximum dose of 200 mg per day.

Preliminary analysis ($N = 19$) indicates that, compared to placebo, treatment with clomipramine was associated with significant improvement in obsessive and compulsive symptoms (we used our own "Obsessive Compulsive Rating," the NIMH Obsessive Compulsive scale, and the Leyton Obsessional Inventory-Child version). Individual treatment responses were marked in about one-third of the children; another third improved moderately. Prediction of drug response to date has been elusive. Change in obsessive-compulsive symptoms was not correlated with initial scores of depression and, for the few patients who were initially depressed, decrease in depression scores during active treatment appeared secondary to improvement of obsessive-compulsive symptoms. Thus, the "anti-obsessional" effect of clomipramine in our experience seemed specific and independent of its antidepressant effect. Moreover, some of the best responders had previously failed to respond to other tricyclic antidepressants.

CONCLUSION

The study of children and adolescents with primary obsessive-compulsive disorder supports the descriptive validity of a distinct disorder that occurs in childhood in a form virtually identical to that seen in adults. Frequently, this disorder is neither preceded by nor associated with obsessional character traits. Despite the variety of rituals, the symptom strategies of children with this disorder are consistent across cases. Precipitating events are unimpressive and developmental histories do not seem to focus on one specific conflict. First-degree relatives reveal no evidence of increased anxiety, depression, or obsessions.

The various neuropsychological investigations taken together suggest central nervous system dysfunction in many of these children. As a group, children with severe primary obsessive-compulsive disorder have a higher than expected frequency of ventricular enlargement. Given neuropsychological and psycho-linguistic tests, they perform very well on tasks of language comprehension, memory and attention, but exhibit specific deficits on tests associated with frontal lobe functions. The high incidence of left-handedness, the spatial processing impairment, and abnormalities of interhemispheric competition provide a hint of cortical dysfunction. However, there is little correlation among measures: the enlarged VBR and neuropsychological deficits do not correlate with each other among subjects, and those few children with mildly abnormal EEGs are not more likely to have neuropsychological impairment or CT scan abnormalities.

These specific neuropsychological findings are more marked than in recent studies with adults. Although our tests were somewhat more specific than those used for the adult patients, it is also possible that childhood onset distinguishes a subgroup with more marked central nervous system dysfunction. Alternatively, children with this disorder may, as they mature, lose some of their neurological signs.

Finally, as in adults, the therapeutic efficacy of clomipramine in childhood obsessive-compulsive disorder appears promising and may ultimately provide a clue to a central physiological abnormality underlying this disorder.

References

Adams P: Obsessive Children. New York, Penguin Books, 1973

Barton Hall M: Obsessive-compulsive states in childhood: their treatment. Arch Dis Child 10:49–59, 1935

Behar D, Rapoport J, Berg C, et al: Computerized tomography and neuropsychological test measures in adolescents with obsessive-compulsive disorder. Am J Psychiatry 141:363–369, 1984

Berman L: The obsessive-compulsive neurosis in children. J Nerv Ment Dis 95:26–39, 1942

Black A: The natural history of obsessional neurosis, in Obsessional States. Edited by Beech HR. London, Methuen, 1974

Bolton D, Collins S, Steinberg D: The treatment of obsessive-compulsive disorder in adolescence: a report of fifteen cases. Br J Psychiatry 142:456–464, 1983

Bornstein B: The analysis of a phobic child. Psychoanal Study Child 3–4:181–226, 1949

Brown F: Heredity in the psychoneuroses. Proceedings of the Royal Society of Medicine 355:785–790, 1942

Campbell M, Rosenbloom S, Perry R, et al: Computerized axial tomography in young autistic children. Am J Psychiatry 139:510–512, 1982

Caparulo B, Cohen D, Rothman S, et al: Computed tomographic brain scanning in children with developmental neuropsychiatric disorders. J Am Acad Child Psychiatry 20:338–357, 1981

Capstick N, Seldrup J: Obsessional states: a study in the relationship between abnormalities occurring at the time of birth and the subsequent development of obsessional symptoms. Acta Psychiatr Scand 56:427–431, 1977

Chetnik M: The treatment of an obsessive-compulsive boy. J Am Acad Child Psychiatry 8:465–484, 1969

Elkins R, Rapoport J, Lipsky A: Obsessive-compulsive disorder of childhood and adolescence. J Am Acad Child Psychiatry 19:511–524, 1980

Fedio P, Cox C, Neophytides A, et al: Neuropsychological profile of Huntington's disease: patients and those at risk, in Advances in Neurology: Huntington's Disease, Vol. 23. Edited by Chase TN, Wexler NS, Barbeau A. New York, Raven Press, 1979

Fine S: Family therapy and a behavioral approach to childhood obsessive-compulsive neurosis. Arch Gen Psychiatry 28:695–697, 1973

Flor-Henry P, Yeudall LT, Koles ZJ, et al: Neuropsychological and power spectral EEG investigations of the obsessive compulsive syndrome. Biol Psychiatry 14:119–130, 1979

Freud S: Notes upon a case of obsessional neurosis, in Complete Psychological Works, standard ed, vol. 10. London, Hogarth Press, 1955

Hafner RJ, Gilchrist P, Bowling J, et al: The treatment of obsessional neurosis in a family setting. Aust NZ J Psychiatry 15:145–151, 1981

Herjanic B, Campbell W: Differentiating psychiatrically disturbed children on the basis of a structured psychiatric interview. J Abnorm Child Psychol 5:127–135, 1977

Hollingsworth C, Tanguay P, Grossman L, et al: Long-term outcome of obsessive compulsive disorder in childhood. J Am Acad Child Psychiatry 19:134–144, 1980

Ingram IM: Obsessional illness in mental hospital patients. Journal of Mental Science 107:1035–1042, 1961

Ingram IM, McAdam WA: The electroencephalogram, obsessional illness and obsessional personality. Journal of Mental Science 106:686–691, 1960

Inouye R: Electroencephalographic study in obsessive compulsive states. Clinical Psychiatry 15:1071–1083, 1973

Insel T, Donnelly E, Lalakea M, et al: Neurological and neuropsychological studies of patients with obsessive-compulsive disorder. Biol Psychiatry 18:741–751, 1983

Insel T, Hoover C, Murphy D: Parents of patients with obsessive-compulsive disorder. Psychol Med 13:807–811, 1983

Janet P: Les Obsessions et al: Psychasthenie, 2nd ed. Paris, Bailliere, 1903

Jessner L: The genesis of a compulsive neurosis. Journal of Hillside Hospital 12:81–95, 1963

Judd L: Obsessive compulsive neurosis in children. Arch Gen Psychiatry 12:136–143, 1965.

Kanner L: Child Psychiatry. Springfield, Ill, Charles C Thomas, 1957

Kringlen E: Obsessional neurotics: a long-term follow-up. Br J Psychiatry 111:709–722, 1965

Lewis A: Problems of obsessional illness. Proceedings of the Royal Society of Medicine 29:325–336, 1936

Lo W: A follow-up study of obsessional neurotics in Hong Kong Chinese. Br J Psychiatry 113:823–832, 1967

O'Connor J: Why I can't get hives: brief strategy therapy with an obsessional child. Fam Process 22:201–209, 1983

Pacella BL, Polantin P, Nagler SH: Clinical and EEG studies in obsessive-compulsive states. Am J Psychiatry 100:830–838, 1944

Pearlson G, Veroff A, McHugh P: The use of computed tomography in psychiatry: recent applications to schizophrenia, manic-depressive illness and dementia syndromes. Johns Hopkins Med J 149:194–202, 1981

Pollitt J: Natural history of obsessional states. Br Med J 1:194–198, 1957

Rapoport J, Elkins R, Mikkelson E: A clinical controlled trial of chlorimipramine in adolescents with obsessive-compulsive disorder. Psychopharmacol Bull 16:61–63, 1980

Rapoport J, Elkins R, Langer D, et al: Childhood obsessive compulsive disorder. Am J Psychiatry 138:1545–1554, 1981

Rockwell FV, Simons DJ: The electroencephalogram and personality organization in the obsessive-compulsive reaction. Archives of Neurology and Psychiatry 57:71–77, 1947

Rosenberg CM: Personality and obsessional neurosis. Br J Psychiatry 113:471–477, 1967

Rutter M, Tizard J, Whitmore K: Education, Health and Behavior. London, Longmans, 1970

Slade PD: Psychometric studies of obsessional illness and obsessional personality, in Obsessional States, Edited by Beech HR. London, Methuen, 1974

Sugiyama T: Clinico-electroencephalographic study on obsessive-compulsive neurosis. Bull Osaka Med Sch 20:95–114, 1974

Warren W: Some relationships between the psychiatry of children and of adults. Journal of Mental Science 106:815–826, 1960

Weinberger D, Torrey E, Neophytides A, et al: Lateral cerebral ventricular enlargement in chronic schizophrenia. Arch Gen Psychiatry 36:735–739, 1979

Weiner I: Behavior therapy in obsessional-compulsive neurosis: treatment of an adolescent boy. Psychotherapy, Theory, Research and Practice 4:27–29, 1967

Welner A, Reich T, Robins E, et al: Obsessive-compulsive neurosis: record, follow-up, and family studies. I. Inpatient record study. Compr Psychiatry 17:527–539, 1976

Wexler BE: Cerebral laterality and psychiatry: a review of the literature. Am J Psychiatry 137:279–291, 1980

3

Behavioral Treatment of Obsessive-Compulsive Ritualizers

Edna B. Foa, Ph.D.
Gail Steketee, M.S.W.

3

Behavioral Treatment of Obsessive-Compulsive Ritualizers

The concept of obsessive-compulsive neurosis has been discussed for over one hundred years. Esquirol (1838) provided the first written account but it was not until the beginning of this century that attempts to arrive at a formal definition were made (e.g., Lewis 1936; Schneider 1925). It is generally agreed that obsessive-compulsive disorder is characterized by recurrent or persistent thoughts, images, impulses, or actions that are accompanied by a sense of subjective compulsion and a desire to resist it. Some patients, identified as obsessionals, suffer from obsessional thoughts, images, or impulses without manifesting overt repetitious actions. However, the majority of obsessive-compulsives complain of both intrusive disturbing thoughts and repetitious, stereotyped actions. Here we will describe a treatment plan designed for the latter patient population.

It is customary to refer to thoughts and images as "obsessions" and to repetitious actions as "compulsions." We find this classification unsatisfactory since it is based on the modality of the symptoms rather than on their function. We suggest instead a distinction that rests on the relationship between anxiety or discomfort and symptoms. Accordingly, thoughts, images, and actions that elicit anxiety or discomfort will be denoted as obsessions. On the other hand, overt behaviors and, more rarely, conditions that are anxiety reducing are termed compulsions.

Compulsions take a variety of forms of which the two most common are washing and checking. Washers are patients who feel contaminated when exposed to certain objects or thoughts; their compulsive behavior consists mostly of excessive ritualistic washing and cleaning. Checkers are patients whose compulsions consist of repetitious checking and/or ritualistic stereotyped actions performed to avoid future "disasters" or punishment. Sometimes rituals are related to anxiety-evoking obsessions in a direct, rational way (e.g., checking to see if the stove is off in order to avoid possible fire); other rituals are not rationally related to the obsessions (e.g., dressing and undressing to prevent one's husband from having an accident).

Both washing and checking can be found in the same patient. For the purposes of outlining a treatment plan, however, they will be considered separately. The following case descriptions are illustrative of each type.

Case 1. Jane is a 30-year-old married woman with two children. She felt contaminated (a nonspecific feeling of being dirty, accompanied by extreme anxiety and discomfort) when in contact with her hometown. Her symptoms began at age 16 when Jane felt contaminated by Christmas ornaments stored in her parents' attic. At first, only these ornaments were disturbing, but within a short period of time, everything that had been in direct or indirect contact with them led to anxiety and a concomitant urge to wash. In addition to feelings of contamination, the ornaments also produced strong feelings of sadness and depression. At the time she applied for treatment, Jane avoided anything associated with her hometown, including family members. These elaborate avoidance efforts, however, proved inadequate to protect her. Jane continuously found herself confronted with items from her hometown, such as chocolates manufactured there and sold in foodstores, where they contaminated other groceries. Such encounters made it necessary for her to engage in extensive washing and cleaning rituals to restore a state of non-contamination. Jane was motivated to seek treatment when her grandmother, whom she loved and had not seen for seven years, became seriously ill. The fear of contamination prevented Jane from visiting her.

Case 2. Mike, a 32-year-old patient, engaged in checking rituals that were triggered by a fear of harming others. When driving he felt compelled to stop the car often to check whether he had run over people, particularly babies. Before flushing the toilet, Mike inspected the commode to be sure that a live insect had not fallen into the toilet—he did not want to be responsible for killing any live creature. In addition, he repeatedly checked the doors, stoves, lights, and windows making sure that all were shut or turned off so that no harm, such as fire or burglary, would befall his family as a result of his "irresponsible" behavior. In particular he worried about the safety of his 15-month-old daughter, repeatedly checking the gate to the basement to be sure that it was locked. He did not carry his daughter while walking on concrete floors in order to avoid killing her by accidentally dropping her. Mike performed these and many other checking rituals for an average of four hours a day. Checking behavior started several months after his marriage, six years before treatment. It increased two years later, when Mike's wife was pregnant with their first child, and continued to worsen over the years.

REVIEW OF TREATMENTS

Obsessive-compulsive disorders have long been considered among the most intractable of the neurotic disorders. As recently as 1961, Breitner (1960) noted that "most of us are agreed that the treatment of obsessional states is one of the most difficult tasks confronting the psychiatrist and many of us consider it hopeless" (p. 32). Traditional psychotherapy has not proven effective in ameliorating obsessive-compulsive symptomatology (Black 1974). In a sample of 90 inpatients, Kringlen (1965) found that only 20 percent had improved at a 13- to 20-year follow-up. Somewhat more favorable results were reported by Grimshaw (1965): 40 percent of an outpatient sample were improved at a one to 14 year follow-up.

Early Forms of Behavioral Treatments

Some improvement in the prognostic picture emerged with the application of treatments derived from learning theories. These methods can be divided into two classes: (1) exposure procedures aimed at reducing the anxiety/discomfort associated with obsessions, and (2) blocking or punishing techniques directed at decreasing the frequency of either obsessive thoughts or ritualistic behaviors.

The most commonly employed exposure treatment was systematic desensitization. Despite initial claims for its efficacy with obsessive-compulsive disorders, a review of the literature indicated that systematic desensitization effected improvement in only 30 to 40 percent of the cases reported (Beech and Vaughan 1978; Cooper et al. 1965). Treatment procedures utilizing prolonged exposure to feared cues (e.g., paradoxical intention, imaginal flooding, satiation and aversion relief) have also been employed with this population. Improvement with these procedures, which have been examined largely through case reports, has not exceeded 60 percent, with the exception of aversion relief, which proved effective to varying degrees for each of five patients.

The second set of treatment methods, blocking or punishing procedures, includes thought stopping, aversion therapy, and covert sensitization. Thought stopping has proven largely ineffective in several case studies. Aversion therapy using electrical shock, the snapping of a rubber band on the wrist or covert sensitization has fared somewhat better. As with the exposure procedures discussed above, our knowledge of the efficacy of blocking techniques is based largely on case reports, which tend to be biased toward positive outcomes.

If, as suggested previously, obsessive-compulsive symptomology is composed of obsessions that evoke anxiety and compulsions that reduce it, then treatment should consist of techniques that decrease anxiety and procedures that suppress compulsions. It follows that the simultaneous use of interventions directed at both obsessions and compulsions would be expected to yield superior results to treatment directed at only one set of symptoms. In the foregoing reports, investigators rarely attempted to match the treatment procedure to the target symptoms. An exception was the use of aversion relief (Marks et al. 1969; Rubin and Merbaum 1971) where compulsive behavior was followed by the administration of electrical shock (blocking), and shock was terminated upon contact with the feared situations (obsessions). Treatment was successful in the two patients who underwent this procedure. Another treatment program that addressed both obsessions and compulsions was exposure and response prevention. This program has proven highly effective and has become the treatment of choice for this disorder. A summary of the research on this procedure follows.

Exposure and Response Prevention

In 1966, Victor Meyer developed a therapeutic program, later labeled "apotrepic therapy" (Meyer et al. 1974), which consisted of two basic components: (1) in vivo exposure to discomfort-evoking stimuli, i.e., placing the patient in the "real life" feared situation, and (2) response prevention, i.e., blocking the compulsive behaviors. The results were impressive; of the 15 patients treated with this program, 10 were rated as much improved or symptom-free, and five were rated as improved. Only two patients relapsed during the follow-up period. At the same time, Stampfl and Levis (1967) formulated a therapeutic procedure consisting of prolonged imaginal exposure to fear-evoking scenes. Called "implosive" therapy, this method was applied primarily to phobics. A few reports with single patients suggested that this therapy might reduce obsessive-compulsive symptoms.

Variants of in vivo exposure and response prevention have been investigated in numerous studies. In contrast to the relatively poor prognosis for obsessive-compulsives with traditional psychotherapy, the overall success rates with these two behavioral procedures were quite high—about 75 percent of patients improved markedly with these treatments (e.g., Marks et al. 1975; Emmelkamp and Kraanen 1977). Slightly better results have been noted with a combination of imaginal and in vivo exposure (Foa and Goldstein 1978). (Extensive reviews have been done by Foa et al. [in press] and Rachman and Hodgson [1980]). At present, exposure in vivo and response prevention, sometimes with the addition of imaginal exposure, have been adopted as the treatment of choice for obsessive-compulsive ritualizers. Is it necessary, however, to apply all three procedures? To answer this question, a series of studies examining the role of each of the three treatment components was conducted.

Differential Effects of Exposure In Vivo and Response Prevention

Since obsessions evoke anxiety, therapy of obsessive-compulsives should include procedures that reduce the obsessional anxiety. To this end, prolonged exposure to an obsessional stimulus has been found to decrease anxiety (Foa and Chambless 1978; Grayson et al. 1982; Nunes and Marks 1975). If rituals are maintained only because of their ability to reduce obsessional anxiety, then—as suggested by Marks (personal communication)—prolonged exposure alone should effectively ameliorate them and response prevention should be unnecessary. Negating this proposition are observations that in some cases prolonged exposure eliminated anxiety, yet compulsive behavior persisted (Marks et al. 1969; Walton and Mather 1963). Perhaps, then, exposure and response prevention operate through separate mechanisms, both of which are required to reduce obsessive-compulsive symptoms successfully.

In a series of five single-case studies, Mills et al. (1973) found that response prevention alone virtually eliminated ritualistic behavior, whereas exposure alone produced either no change or an increase in compulsions and subjective urges to ritualize. (Anxiety was not measured in this study.) However, contact with the discomfort-evoking stimuli was brief, and, therefore, the failure of exposure to reduce compulsions may have been due to inadequate exposure. In two additional series of single-case experiments (Turner et al. 1979; Turner et al. 1980), response prevention decreased ritualistic behaviors but affected anxiety only minimally. Exposure ameliorated anxiety but did not enhance the efficacy of response prevention in reducing ritualistic behavior.

In a series of studies, we extended these case reports to investigate the short- and long-term effects of both exposure and response prevention (Foa et al. manuscript in preparation). In one experiment 32 obsessive-compulsives with washing rituals were treated

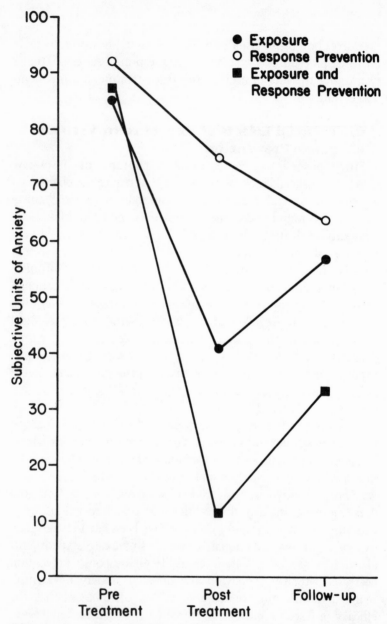

Figure 1 Mean Highest Subjective Anxiety Levels During Exposure Test for the Three Treatment Groups Before and After Treatment and at Follow-up

with 15 sessions (over three weeks) of in vivo exposure only, response prevention only, or the combination of these two procedures. The results indicated that immediately after treatment deliberate exposure decreased anxiety to contaminants more than did response prevention. Ritualistic behavior, in turn, was ameliorated more by response prevention than by exposure. The group who received both treatments benefitted most on measures of anxiety associated with contaminants and time spent washing (Figures 1 and 2). At a nine-month follow-up the superiority of the combined group was retained on measures of obsessive anxiety. With regard to compulsions, at follow-up the three groups did not

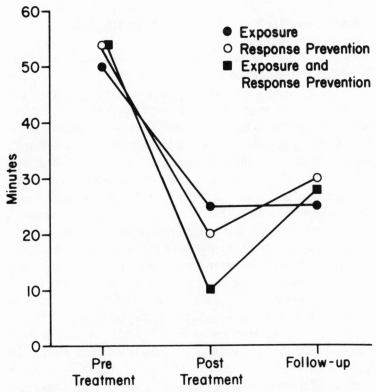

Figure 2 Self-monitored Washing Time for the Three Treatment Groups Before and After Treatment and at Follow-up

Table 1 Exposure In Vivo Versus Combined Imaginal and In Vivo Exposure
at Post-treatment

	Outcome			
	Much Improved	Improved	Failures	Total
Imaginal and in vivo exposure	14	7	2	23
In vivo exposure	14	12	0	26
Total	28	19	2	49

differ on time spent washing; however, on other measures of
compulsions—urges to ritualize and severity of main ritual—the
combined group improved the most.

Exposure In Vivo Versus Exposure in Imagination

As stated earlier, imaginal exposure has been employed in the
treatment of obsessive-compulsives. Some authors reported success
with this procedure (Frankl 1960, Stampfl 1967); others have
found it ineffective (Marks et al. 1969; Rachman et al. 1970;
Wolpe 1964). The literature suggests that actual confrontation
with feared situations is superior to exposure in fantasy with
simple phobics (e.g., Emmelkamp and Wessels 1975; Mathews
1978; Marks 1978). It stands to reason, therefore, that when
obsessive fear is evoked primarily by tangible cues (e.g., urine,
dirt), exposure in vivo will fare better than imaginal exposure.

For many patients, however, anxiety is generated both by
tangible cues from their environment and by anticipation of harm
that might ensue from confrontation with these cues; the latter
(e.g., death, disease, house burning down) can be presented only in
fantasy. For example, the patient who is afraid of running over
someone and therefore constantly rechecks his path, can be
exposed in vivo to his fears by requiring him to drive without
checking. Obviously, the exposure session will not include the
actual hitting of a pedestrian and leaving him behind to die
because of failure to check carefully. Exposure to such a "disaster"
can be accomplished only in imagination.

If it is important to match the content of the exposure situation

Table 2 Exposure In Vivo Versus Combined Imaginal and In Vivo Exposure at Follow-up

	Outcome			
	Much Improved	Improved	Failures	Total
Imaginal and in vivo exposure	15	1	5	21
In vivo exposure	12	7	6	25
Total	27	8	11	46

to a patient's internal fear model (Lang 1977), then those who fear disastrous consequences (which cannot be produced in reality) should improve more with the addition of imaginal exposure. To study this issue, data from 49 obsessive-compulsives were analyzed (Steketee et al. 1982). Twenty-six patients (nine checkers and 17 washers) received 10 to 15 daily two-hour sessions of exposure in vivo. Twenty-three patients (seven checkers and 16 washers) received 90 minutes of imaginal exposure followed by 30 minutes of in vivo exposure.

On the basis of percent change scores of assessor rated obsessions and compulsions, patients were divided into three groups: (1) "much improved" were those who showed treatment gains of 70 percent or more; (2) "improved" were those who evidenced treatment gains of 31 percent to 69 percent; and (3) "failures" were those who improved 30 percent or less. The results for post-treatment and for follow-up (mean, 11 months) are given in Tables 1 and 2, respectively.

These results suggest that the addition of imaginal exposure to in vivo exposure does not affect short-term treatment gains but does increase on the maintenance of such gains. When data at post-treatment and at follow-up were cross tabulated, only 19 percent of patients who received imaginal exposure lost gains over time, in contrast to the 40 percent relapse rate among those who received exposure in vivo only. (The χ^2 value was significant at the .08 level). It appears, then, that when feared disasters are not directly addressed the reduction of discomfort to environmental (concrete) situations tends to be temporary, perhaps because the core of the fear, i.e., concern with future catastrophes, has not changed. It is important to note that not all patients who did not receive imaginal exposure lost gains at follow-up. Perhaps patients who can generate their entire internal fear model (including fears of disasters) when presented with concrete cues do not require the addition of imaginal exposure.

In summary, the results of the studies discussed above argue for the use of deliberate in vivo exposure in combination with response prevention in the treatment of obsessive-compulsives. They also suggest that imaginal exposure be added for those who manifest fears of future catastrophes.

CLINICAL IMPLEMENTATION OF TREATMENT

The treatment program consists of three stages: an information gathering period, an intensive exposure/response prevention phase, and a follow-up maintenance period. These are summarized below.

Information Gathering Period

The goals of the first interviews with the patient are two-fold: establishing a diagnosis and collecting information pertinent to treatment planning. First the nature of the obsessions must be explored. The vast majority of obsessive-compulsives describe external cues that evoke anxiety. The therapist should solicit highly specific information about these cues in an attempt to identify the sources of concern. Such identification is important but often quite difficult because contamination "travels" and neutral objects become contaminants through contact (which may be quite remote) with the source of contamination. It is impossible, for example, to understand the patient who fears touching leather items, animals, and men without the knowledge that all of these are contaminated only because they are associated with "maleness" (i.e., leather from male animals). Ascertaining the source of fear is important not only for comprehending the patient's conceptual structure but also for determining the situations to which patients must be exposed. If treatment omits direct confrontation with the source of fear, a relapse often occurs.

Anxiety/discomfort may be generated by internal cues, including thoughts, images, or impulses that are disturbing, shameful, disgusting, or horrifying. Examples of these cues are number sequences, impulses to stab one's child (triggered, in turn, by external cues such as knives or scissors), thoughts that one's spouse may have an auto acident on the way home, and images of having sex with Christ. Some patients are reluctant to disclose their obsessions, but they can usually be encouraged by direct questions, a matter-of-fact attitude, and reassurance that most normal individuals also have unwanted thoughts.

Often, the external and internal obsessional cues are associated with anticipated harm, which for some patients may constitute the primary cause for discomfort. Although the specific content of the feared disasters varies from patient to patient, most washers fear that contamination will result in disease, physical debilitation, or death to themselves or others. Most checkers fear being responsible for an error that will lead to physical harm (e.g., leaving the stove on and thereby burning the house down) or to psychological harm (e.g., setting the table incorrectly and being criticized by a significant other; writing "I am a homosexual" on a check and thereby losing others' respect). Those with repeating rituals are typically concerned that their upsetting thoughts will come to pass (e.g., an accident happening, losing control and stabbing someone, punishment from God). The information about the external fear cues determines the exposure in vivo program; knowledge about the internal cues and feared disasters constitutes the basis for imaginal exposure.

Both active and passive forms of avoidance behavior are exhibited by obsessive-compulsives. Whenever possible obsessive-compulsives, like phobics, seek to circumvent passively situations that provoke discomfort. Most avoidance patterns are clear cut (e.g. refraining from using public toilets, shaking hands, touching garbage, using the stove, or taking out the trash). Sometimes, however, they can be quite subtle. Examples include sidestepping brown spots on the sidewalk (possible dog feces), touching doorknobs at their less-used base with fingers only (to be washed later), sitting forward on chairs to avoid the spot that others usually contact, wearing only slip-on shoes to avoid having to touch laces or buckles. It is important to identify avoidance behaviors and to prohibit them during treatment since even minor avoidances prevent full exposure to the fear cues and therefore may serve to maintain that fear. Additionally, retention of avoidance patterns may reinforce the patient's belief that they protect him from the "danger" inherent in exposure.

Active forms of avoidance, i.e., ritualistic behavior, have already been described. They consist of washing, cleaning (including wiping with alcohol or spraying with Lysol), checking, repeating actions, placing objects in a precise order, and repeatedly requesting reassurance. They also include cognitive rituals, such as praying, thinking "good" thoughts, and listing events mentally. The function of rituals is to reduce anxiety associated with the obsessions. The relationship of each ritual to fear and to passive avoidance behaviors should be ascertained. When such a relationship is lacking, one should question the diagnosis of obsessive-compulsive disorder and consider the possibility of a psychotic disorder.

On the basis of information about the internal and external fear cues, the feared harm and the active and passive avoidance behaviors, a treatment program can be designed.

THE TREATMENT PROGRAM

Exposure

For external fears in vivo exposure is recommended over imaginal techniques (Rabavilas et al. 1976; Emmelkamp and Wessels 1975). Research has determined that for most patients the speed with which the most anxiety provoking object is confronted matters little (Hodgson et al. 1972). But since patients prefer gradual exposure, we usually employ a five or six step hierarchy. For example, a patient who feared contamination from feces, urine, sweat, and other body secretions was first asked to hold doorknobs continuously, especially those to public restrooms. In the second session, discarded newspapers were added to the doorknobs. In later sessions, he was introduced to sweat and toilet seats.

application of exposure and response prevention treatment for a patient with washing rituals. The preliminary interviews with Jane revealed that her obsessions were focused primarily on external objects. Because of the absence of anticipated harm, the treatment program did not include imaginal exposure. In preparation for treatment, we wrote to Jane's mother, who lived in the contaminated hometown, and requested that she mail us objects from home including clothing, books, and ornaments from the attic. These were kept away from Jane until the beginning of treatment.

In the first session, Jane and the therapist went into the supermarket to purchase groceries located near the counter where the chocolate from her hometown was situated. She touched these items to her face, hair, and clothing; anxiety increased to 50 SUDs (subjective units of disturbance, ranging from zero to 100) and declined to 20 SUDs after 90 minutes. Jane continued the exposure at home after the session, contaminating her entire house, including her bed, closets, drawers, etc. On the second day she brought into the session books, kitchen utensils, and some clothes that she had been avoiding because of their indirect contact with contaminants. On the third day, Jane handled and ate chocolates from her hometown. In this session her high level of anxiety necessitated some coaxing from the therapist, starting with brief contact by one finger and gradually increasing it until she was able to touch the chocolate with her entire hand. In the next session, Jane was required to wear the clothes sent from home. In subsequent sessions, she wore her mother's clothes and touched the ornaments. Anxiety to the latter contaminant increased to 90 SUDs and required three hours to habituate to a level of 40 SUDs. The remainder of treatment concentrated on contact with various items from home. In the last (fifteenth) session the therapist accompanied Jane to her hometown where they went to her attic to handle all of the objects that still provoked some discomfort. She brought some of them back with her so that exposure to the source of contamination could continue.

Throughout this intensive three-week program, Jane was instructed to refrain from washing her hands entirely and to limit her showering to 10 minutes every fifth day. To reinforce maintenance of her gains she was advised to return to her hometown every two weeks for a period of three months. A follow-up eight years later indicated that Jane's improvement had been maintained.

TREATMENT OF A CHECKER: THE CASE OF MIKE

Mike, the patient with the checking rituals described earlier, feared both external situations and the disasters that might ensue if he failed to ritualize. Treatment, therefore, included both imaginal and in vivo exposure, with the addition of response prevention. The first scene that Mike was asked to imagine was as follows: Mike was at school where he teaches. He failed to check the toilet bowl before flushing it. A school child came looking for his gerbil in the bathroom where the cage was kept. The cage was empty and the child cried, worrying that the gerbil fell into the toilet. Mike feared that he indeed flushed the gerbil down the toilet since he failed to check. During the image, his reported anxiety climbed to 80 SUDs and gradually diminished to 30 SUDs. In vivo exposure during the first session involved flushing toilets in public restrooms with eyes closed. The homework assignment was not to check the toilet at home before flushing it.

In the second scene Mike imagined that he has forgotten to check the windows and doors; a burglar entered and stole his wife's jewelry. She blamed him for the theft. In vivo, Mike was required to close doors and windows, checking briefly only once. Next, Mike was asked to imagine that he dropped his baby daughter on a concrete floor because he did not hold her properly. She was hospitalized for injuries and both his wife and parents accused him of carelessness. In vivo exposure consisted of walking with his daughter on a concrete floor until his anxiety reduced. In subsequent scenes Mike fantasized driving over a bump on the expressway and then worrying that he had run over someone. A police car pulled him over and charged him with a hit-and-run accident. His homework required city driving among pedestrians and potholes without stopping and without checking his rearview mirror or retracing his path.

At a three-year follow-up, Mike reported 10 minutes of checking per day in contrast to four hours before treatment. Most of the excessive checking was done in the classroom in an attempt to prevent papers from being mixed up; some brief unnecessary checking of doors and windows at home also persisted.

TREATMENT COMPLICATIONS

Noncompliance

When confronted with a description of the exposure/response prevention program, about 25 percent of obsessive-compulsives who approach behavioral treatment decline to participate. This attrition process leaves in treatment only the motivated patients. Nevertheless, a few of them fail to abide by the agreed-upon rules and a larger number try to bend them. Failure to resist rituals and persistance in avoidance patterns lead inevitably to a poor outcome.

It is unusual for an obsessive-compulsive patient to conceal ritualistic activity from the therapist. When this happens, the patient should be confronted with the implications of the failure to comply for treatment outcome. If noncompliance persists, therapy should be discontinued with the understanding that the patient may return when he or she is prepared to follow the treatment regimen. Continuance under conditions in which failure is likely to occur will leave the patient hopeless about future prospects for improvement.

Another motivational problem is posed by individuals who carry out exposure exercises without ritualizing but continue to engage in passive avoidance patterns. The persistence of such behaviors hinders habituation of anxiety to feared situations and may leave the patient with the erroneous belief that this avoidance protects him from harm. Failure to give up avoidance patterns also calls for a reevaluation of continuation in treatment.

Familial Patterns

Family members have typically experienced intense frustration due to the patient's symptoms. It is not surprising that some are impatient, expecting treatment to result in rapid and complete symptom remission. Conversely, family members may continue to "protect" the patient from previously upsetting situations, thus reinforcing avoidance behaviors. Years of accommodation to the patient's peculiar requests have established communication patterns that are difficult to break. The above familial patterns may hinder progress in treatment and interfere with maintenance of gains, thus requiring therapeutic intervention.

Functioning Without Symptoms

Many obsessive-compulsives have become socially and occupationally nonfunctional as their symptoms occupied an increasing proportion of their life. Successful treatment leaves them with a considerable void in their daily routine. Assistance in acquiring new skills and in planning both social and occupational activities should be the focus of follow-up therapy in such cases.

FAILURES AND RELAPSES

The interference of depression with treatment outcome has been widely noted (e.g., Rachman and Hodgson 1980; Foa et al. 1983b). Patients who exhibited severely depressed moods prior to treatment tended not to benefit from treatment and were particularly prone to relapse at follow-up. The alleviation of depression by pharmacological and psychological means should be considered for these patients before beginning behavioral treatment.

An anxious mood at the outset of therapy was also found related to patients' response to treatment but in a somewhat different manner than depression. Those with mild anxiety were more likely to succeed; but those with high anxiety, unlike high depression, were equally likely to succeed or to fail.

A further stumbling block in treatment may be the patient's belief system regarding the likelihood that the feared consequences will in fact materialize. Foa (1979) observed that those who firmly believed that their worst fears would come to pass if they failed to protect themselves by ritualizing did not habituate to feared contaminants, either within an exposure session or across sessions. Unfortunately, reliable or valid measures of the degree of conviction have not yet been developed and thus the validity of these observations has not been tested in a controlled manner.

CONCLUDING COMMENTS

Innovations in behavioral treatment, particularly exposure and response prevention, have profoundly improved the prognostic picture for obsessive-compulsives. However, patients rarely find themselves entirely symptom free at the completion of this regimen. Maintenance of gains is problematic for about 20 percent of patients (Foa et al. 1983b). Relapse is most common among those patients who are only partially improved at the end of treatment. The implementation of drugs, specifically antidepressants, in combination with behavioral treatment may prove useful for those who manifest severely depressed moods at the beginning of treatment. More importantly, we need to develop maintenance programs that focus on the patient's interpersonal and occupational adjustment and provide support in the struggle to progress from a nonfunctional to a healthy lifestyle.

References

Beech HR, Vaughan M: Behavioral treatment of obsessional states. New York, John Wiley and Sons, 1978

Black A: The natural history of obsessional neurosis, in Obsessional States. Edited by Beech HR. London, Methuen, 1974

Breitner C: Drug therapy in obsessional states and other psychiatric problems. Diseases of the Nervous System (Supplement) 21:31–35, 1960

Cooper JE, Gelder MG, Marks IM: Results of behavior therapy in 77 psychiatric patients. Br Med J 1:1222–1225, 1965

Emmelkamp PMG, Kraanen J: Therapist-controlled exposure in vivo: a comparison with obsessive-compulsive patients. Behav Res Ther 15:491–495, 1977

Emmelkamp PMG, Wessels H: Flooding in imagination and flooding in vivo: a comparison with agoraphobics. Behav Res Ther 13:7–15, 1975

Esquirol JED: Des Maladies Mentales, Vol. 2. Paris, Bailliere, 1838

Foa EB: Failure in treating obsessive-compulsives. Behav Res Ther 17:169–176, 1979

Foa EB, Chambless DL: Habituation of subjective anxiety during flooding in imagery. Behav Res Ther 16:392–399, 1978

Foa EB, Goldstein A: Continuous exposure and complete response prevention in the treatment of obsessive-compulsive neurosis. Behavior Therapy 9:821–829, 1978

Foa EB, Grayson J, Steketee GS, et al: Success and failure in the behavioral treatment of obsessive-compulsives. J Consult Clin Psychol 51:287–297, 1983a.

Foa EB, Steketee G, Grayson JB, et al: Treatment of obsessive-compulsives: When do we fail? in Failures in Behavior Therapy. Edited by Foa EB, Emmelkamp PMG. New York, Wiley, 1983b

Foa EB, Steketee G, Grayson JB, et al: Deliberate exposure and blocking of obsessive-compulsive rituals: immediate and long term effects. Manuscript in preparation

Foa EB, Steketee GS, Ozarow BJ: Behavior therapy with obsessive-compulsives: from theory to treatment, in Obsessive-Compulsive Disorders: Psychological and Pharmacological Treatments. Edited by Mavissakalian M. New York, Plenum Press (in press)

Frankl VE: Paradoxical intention: a logotherapeutic technique. Am J Psychother 14:520–525, 1960

Grayson JB, Foa EB, Steketee G: Habituation during exposure treatment: distraction versus attention-focusing. Behav Res Ther 20:323–328, 1982

Grimshaw L: The outcome of obsessional disorder, a follow-up study of 100 cases. Br J Psychiatry 111:1051–1056, 1965

Hodgson RJ, Rachman S, Marks IM: The treatment of chronic obsessive-compulsive neurosis: follow-up and further findings. Behav Res Ther 10:181–189, 1972

Kringlen E: Obsessional neurotics, a long-term follow-up. Br J Psychiatry 111:709–722, 1965

Lang PJ: Imagery in therapy: an information processing analysis of fear. Behavior Therapy 8:862–886, 1977

Lewis AJ: Problems of obsessional illness. Proceedings of the Royal Society of Medicine 29:325–336, 1936

Marks IM: Behavioral psychotherapy of adult neurosis, in Handbook of Psychotherapy and Behavior Change. Edited by Garfield S, Bergin A. New York, John Wiley & Sons, 1978

Marks IM, Crowe E, Drewe E, et al: Obsessive-compulsive neurosis in identical twins. Br J Psychiatry 15:991–998, 1969

Marks IM, Hodgson R, Rachman S: Treatment of chronic obsessive-compulsive neurosis by in vivo exposure, a 2-year follow-up and issues in treatment. Br J Psychiatry 127:349–364, 1975

Mathews AM: Fear-reduction research and clinical phobias. Psychol Bull 85:390–404, 1978

Meyer V: Modification of expectations in cases with obsessional rituals. Behav Res Ther 4:273–280, 1966

Meyer V, Levy R, Schnurer A: A behavioural treatment of obsessive-compulsive disorders, in Obsessional States. Edited by Beech HR. London, Methuen, 1974

Mills HL, Agras WS, Barlow DH, et al: Compulsive rituals treated by response prevention. Arch Gen Psychiatry 28:524–529, 1973

Nunes JS, Marks IM: Feedback of true heart rate during exposure in vivo. Arch Gen Psychiatry 32:933–936, 1975

Rabavilas AD, Boulougouris JC, Stefanis C: Duration of flooding sessions in the treatment of obsessive-compulsive patients. Behav Res Ther 14:349–355, 1976

Rachman S, DeSilva P, Roper G: The spontaneous decay of compulsive urges. Behav Res Ther 14:445–453, 1976

Rachman S, Hodgson R: Obsessions and Compulsions. Englewood Cliffs, NJ, Prentice Hall, 1980

Rachman S, Hodgson R, Marzillier J: Treatment of an obsessional-compulsive disorder by modelling. Behav Res Ther 8:383–392, 1970

Rachman S, Marks IM, Hodgson R: The treatment of obsessive-compulsive neurotics by modelling and flooding in vivo. Behav Res Ther 11:463–471, 1973

Rubin RD, Merbaum M: Self-imposed punishment versus desensitization, in Advances in Behavior Therapy 1969. Edited by Rubin RD, Fensterheim H, Lazarus AA, et al. New York, Academic Press, 1971, pp 85–91

Schneider K: Schwangs zus Tande un Schizophrenie. Archiv für Psychiatrie und Nervenkrankheiten 74:93–107, 1925

Stampfl T: Implosive therapy: the theory, the subhuman analogue, the strategy and the technique, Part 1. The theory, in Behavior Modification Techniques in the Treatment of Emotional Disorders. Edited by Armitage SG. Battle Creek, Mich, V.A. Publications, 1967

Stampfl TG, Levis DJ: Essentials of implosive therapy: a learning-theory-based psychodynamic behavioral therapy. J Abnorm Psychol 72:496–503, 1967

Steketee GS, Foa EB, Grayson JB: Recent advances in the behavioral treatment of obsessive-compulsives. Arch Gen Psychiatry 39:1365–1371, 1982

Turner SM, Hersen M, Bellack AS, et al: Behavioral treatment of obsessive-compulsive neurosis. Behav Res Ther 17:95–106, 1979

Turner SM, Hersen M, Bellack AS, et al: Behavioral and pharmacological treatment of obsessive-compulsive disorders. J Nerv Ment Dis 168:651–657, 1980

Walton D, Mather MD: The application of learning principles to the treatment of obsessive-compulsive states in the acute and chronic phases of illness. Behav Res Ther 1:163–174, 1963

Wolpe J: Behaviour therapy in complex neurotic states. Br J Psychiatry 110:28–34, 1964

4

The Psychopharmacologic Treatment of Obsessive-Compulsive Disorder

Thomas R. Insel, M.D.
Edward A. Mueller, M.D.

4

The Psychopharmacologic Treatment of Obsessive-Compulsive Disorder

Of all psychiatric conditions, obsessive-compulsive disorder has generally been considered one of the most refractory to treatment. Patients with this disorder frequently present with symptoms seemingly laden with unconscious symbolism and dynamic meaning. Yet psychodynamic treatments, particularly if they are loosely structured and nondirective, rarely reduce the symptoms. Behavioral approaches fare much better, especially if they include exposure and response prevention (see Chapter 3). Unfortunately behavior therapy benefits only a fraction of obsessional patients. Those obsessive-compulsive disorder patients without avoidant behavior and those without rituals (i.e. pure obsessionals) provide very little that can be approached with behavior therapy. Many patients with obsessive-compulsive disorder may have secondary depressions and these patients also may be less responsive to behavior therapy (Foa 1979). Finally, many patients who might be excellent candidates for behavior therapy refuse the treatment. Given the low efficacy of psychodynamic treatments and the restricted applicability of behavior therapy, the pharmacologic approach has recently become a focus for clinical researchers interested in treating the entire spectrum of this disorder.

As might be expected with such a chronic and treatment refractory condition, a wide variety of medications have been given to obsessive-compulsive disorder patients. There have been case reports documenting responses to lithium (Stern and Jenike 1983), phenelzine (Annesley 1969; Jain et al. 1970; Isberg 1981), tranylcypromine (Jenike 1981), and clonidine (Knesevich 1982). All of these reports are limited to only one or two patients and the treatments are not placebo controlled, so the most one can conclude in each case is that more study is needed. Particularly because obsessive-compulsive disorder is uncommon and possibly heterogeneous (Insel 1982), the validity of generalizing from a single case is limited.

Reports of several more extensive uncontrolled medication trials have been published. Jenike and coworkers (1983) described a series of obsessive-compulsive disorder patients treated with MAO inhibitors. He reported improvement only in those patients with a history of panic attacks. Ananth (1976) has suggested that neuroleptics are useful during acute exacerbations of obsessive-compulsive disorder. Benzodiazepines have also been investigated for

Table 1 Double-Blind Studies in Adults with Obsessive-Compulsive Disorders

Study	N*	Design†	Improvement in Obsessive-Compulsive Symptoms
Thoren et al. 1980	24 (I)	Parallel CMI vs NOR vs PLAC	CMI > PLAC (5 weeks) NOR not > PLAC
Marks et al. 1980	40 (I then O)	Parallel CMI vs PLAC 4 weeks then behavior Rx	CMI > PLAC (4-week self rating only) CMI + behav. Rx > PLAC + behav. Rx (depressed subgroup only)
Montgomery 1980	14	Crossover CMI vs PLAC	CMI > PLAC (4 weeks)
Ananth et al. 1981	20 (I + O)	Parallel CMI vs AMI	CMI not AMI improved from baseline (4 weeks)
Insel et al. 1983a	13 (I + O)	Crossover CMI vs CLG; PLAC control	CMI > CLG (4 + 6 weeks) PLAC ineffective

*N = number of patients, I = inpatients, O = outpatients.
†CMI = clomipramine, NOR = nortriptyline, PLAC = placebo, AMI = amitriptyline, CLG = clorgyline.

obsessional patients (Rao 1964; Orvin 1967), although the extent to which they reduce obsessional symptoms is not stated in these reports.

The most promising developments, however, have been with the tricyclic antidepressant clomipramine (Anafranil, Ciba-Geigy). Although clomipramine is not yet available for general clinical use in the United States, it has been one of the most widely used antidepressants elsewhere. As early as 1969, Lopez-Ibor reported that intravenous clomipramine reduced the obsessional symptoms of depressed patients (Lopez-Ibor 1969). During the 1970s a series of confirmatory but uncontrolled studies from England and Canada extended this initial observation to oral clomipramine for patients with primary obsessive-compulsive disorder (Capstick 1977; Rack 1977; Ananth et al. 1979). More recently, a group of carefully controlled double blind studies using clomipramine (Table 1) have been published (Thoren et al. 1980; Marks et al. 1980; Montgomery 1980; Ananth et al. 1981; Insel et al. 1983).

We can draw several conclusions from these studies. First, clomipramine is more effective than placebo in reducing obsessional symptoms (Thoren et al. 1980; Marks et al. 1980; Montgomery 1980; Insel et al. 1983a). Combining the data from all of the studies in Table 1, of 64 obsessive-compulsive disorder patients treated with clomipramine, approximately two-thirds improved significantly as measured by blind clinical ratings. Second, clomipramine is more effective than the MAO inhibitor clorgyline (Insel et al. 1983a) and possibly more effective than the tricyclic antidepressant amitriptyline (Ananth et al. 1981). In the study by Thoren et al. (1980), the effects of nortriptyline were intermediate between placebo and clomipramine, and not significantly different from either. Third, the beneficial effects of clomipramine are evident in pure obsessionals as well as ritualizers (Thoren et al. 1980; Insel et al. 1983a). Finally, it appears that the pharmacologic reduction of obsessional symptoms may require at least 4 to 6 weeks of treatment (with full benefit as late as 12 weeks) and that the drug dose for these effects is in the range used to treat depression (75–300 mg/day).

Is Obsessive-Compulsive Disorder a Form of Depression?

Given these results with the antidepressant clomipramine, one might wonder if obsessive-compulsive disorder is a variant of affective illness. Not so long ago the syndrome of obsessive-compulsive disorder was labelled "religious melancholy" (Maudsley 1895). Even within our modern nosology, symptoms such as guilt, indecisiveness, low self-esteem, anxiety, exhaustion, and sleep disturbance are common to both obsessive-compulsive disorder and depression. Furthermore, recent studies have demonstrated that many of the "biological markers" once thought specific to primary affective illness are prevalent in patients with obsessive-compulsive disorder. The dexamethasone suppression test (Insel et al. 1982b; Asberg et al. 1982; Cottraux et al., in press), rapid eye movement (REM) latency on the sleep EEG (Insel et al. 1982c), and the growth hormone response to clonidine (Siever et al. 1983) have all been reported to be abnormal in obsessive-compulsive disorder patients. For each of these measures, the findings resemble those previously reported with depressives, and yet the findings appear to be present in obsessional patients both with and without overt depressive symptomatology.

The relationship between obsessive-compulsive disorder and affective illness is certainly complex. Not only are several symptoms and biologic features common to both syndromes, but one frequently finds patients who appear to suffer from both obsessional disorder and depression. In our own series of obsessional patients, nearly half report a history of a major depression. Welner and associates (1976) in a chart review of 150 cases of obsessionalism found only 30 without depression, in 77 cases depression was either concurrent or subsequent to obsessions and compulsions, and in the remainder depression preceded the obsessions. Goodwin and coworkers (1969) concluded from a review of outcome studies of obsessional disorder that depression was the most common complication of this illness. Indeed, many chronic obsessionals may only present for treatment when they become acutely depressed.

Although several investigators have characterized the obsessions of patients with primary depression (see Chapter 1), there has been little systematic study of the role of affective symptoms in obsessive-compulsive disorder. As with any disorder that is chronic and interferes with functioning, some dysphoria seems entirely predictable. What complicates matters is that changes in mood may modify the obsessional symptoms. From his retrospective study of 398 primary depressives, Gittleson concluded, "During an attack of depressive psychosis, those with pre-morbid obsessions are just as likely to lose them as those without them are to gain them. For both the chance is 1 in 4" (1966, p. 707). The great majority of obsessive-compulsive disorder patients continue to have the obsessional symptoms in spite of ensuing depressions (Gittleson 1966). Such patients are given a diagnosis of primary obsessive-compulsive disorder and secondary depression. The primary-secondary distinction in this case refers to the temporal sequence of onset. This rank ordering may be misleading, however, as the depression may be disabling and may even be the primary reason for seeking treatment. In that fraction of patients who lose their obsessional symptoms as the affective symptoms emerge, one wonders if the rituals or ruminations served as a "depressive equivalent." Certainly the biological marker studies would be consistent with this notion. In addition, an increased incidence of affective illness has been reported in first degree relatives of obsessive-compulsive disorder patients (Black 1974; Insel et al. 1983b; but also see Coryell 1981). Rare reports of cyclic obsessive-compulsive disorder would also support a relationship to affective illness (Mayer-Gross et al. 1960). Possibly then, even those obsessionals who have never been overtly depressed might be suffering from an affective rather than an anxiety disorder.

Before leaping to such a conclusion, one must remember that major differences remain in both the profile of symptoms and the clinical course of obsessive-compulsive disorder and affective illness. Obsessionals complain of fears, rituals, and intrusive thoughts (which when aggressive are usually directed at others) in contrast to patients with depression who are more likely to present with hopelessness and suicidal thoughts. Depressed patients may ruminate, but these repetitive thoughts are usually of a single past experience (e.g., "if only I hadn't left my job, none of this would have happened to me") rather than having the intrusive, ego-dystonic, future oriented renewable character of a true obsession (e.g., "when I see an ax, I'm afraid I'll use it to decapitate my mother"). Obsessive-compulsive disorder frequently begins in childhood and usually has a chronic course. Affective illness usually begins in adulthood and follows an episodic course (Coryell 1981).

Given the pure culture, one can conclude that obsessive-compulsive disorder is not a form of affective illness. In practice, there is a complex overlapping of both symptoms and biologic features. Obsessive-compulsive disorder is frequently complicated by depression. And there may be a common genetic predisposition for the two syndromes. We still do not know (1) if some obsessive-compulsive disorder patients fail to manifest typical affective symptoms when depressed and (2) if depression continues to recur episodically following the successful treatment of obsessive-compulsive disorder.

CLOMIPRAMINE: ANTIOBSESSIONAL OR ANTIDEPRESSANT?

If obsessive-compulsive disorder is frequently complicated by affective symptoms, is clomipramine simply relieving depression? Marks et al. (1980) reported that only those obsessive-compulsive disorder patients with high ratings of depression respond to the drug. This observation has not been entirely corroborated by others (Thoren et al. 1980; Montgomery 1980). In our own initial study of clomipramine (Insel et al. 1983a), patients with the lowest depression ratings (Hamilton Depression Rating Score, <10) improved as much as those with high ratings of depression (Hamilton Depression Rating Score >20). Furthermore, in a single case treated when euthymic (Hamilton Depression Rating Scale, 6) and subsequently when depressed (Hamilton Depression Rating Scale, 26), the decrease in obsessional symptoms was identical (Insel et al. 1982a). Our data then suggest that a high depression rating is not a prerequisite for response to clomipramine. This, however, does not exclude the possibility that the drug is working as an antidepressant. If obsessional disorder represents a "depressive equivalent," then patients may not manifest the typical signs and symptoms measured on a depression rating scale.

If the clomipramine effect in obsessive-compulsive disorder were purely an antidepressant response, then one might expect that other antidepressants would be equally effective. This is not the case. As mentioned above, clorgyline, nortriptyline, and amitriptyline—all excellent antidepressants—do not appear to be effective for obsessive-compulsive disorder. In our own experience with three depressed obsessional patients who received electroconvulsive therapy (ECT), their depressive symptoms resolved but the obsessional symptoms were unchanged.

Taken together, the improvement in obsessional symptoms in the absence of clinically evident depression and the apparent selectivity of clomipramine relative to other antidepressants would suggest that this drug reduces obsessional symptoms independently from its effects on depression. Marks (1983), on the other hand, has argued against a specific antiobsessional effect by suggesting that drugs such as clomipramine are "patholytic," reducing a broad range of affective and anxiety related symptoms (also see Mavissakalian and Michelson 1983).

If clomipramine were specifically antiobsessional then the drug should affect measures of arousal and habituation, two psychophysiologic variables hypothesized to be abnormal and possibly etiologic in obsessional states (Beech and Perigault 1974). In our own study comparing clomipramine and clorgyline, we investigated psychophysiologic responsiveness during the placebo and each of the active drug phases to try to assess changes that might be both specific to clomipramine and correlated with treatment response. The full description of this study has appeared elsewhere (Zahn et al., in press). Briefly, both clorgyline and clomipramine reduced skin conductance level at rest. However, under aversive conditions, such as during a period of unpredictable 100 db tones or during a two-flash discrimination task, drug related differences in psychophysiologic responsiveness emerged. During the placebo and clorgyline conditions, obsessive-compulsive disorder patients showed a marked increase in the number and amplitude of the orienting responses following the 100 db tones and a marked increase in skin conductance during the two flash threshold task. These same subjects, when taking clomipramine, showed very little increase in psychophysiologic activity during these identical experimental challenges. Furthermore, when clomipramine treated patients were divided into more improved and less improved subgroups on the basis of changes in obsessional ratings, the more improved subjects showed significantly less psychophysiologic responsivity when stressed with the tone or the two-flash-threshold tasks. While it is difficult to generalize from laboratory paradigms to naturalistic threats, these results suggest that at least some aspects of response to an aversive stimulus correlate with the ratings of clinical improvement with clomipramine. Such studies of habituation and psychophysiologic responsivity may ultimately reveal an important factor in the improvement of obsessional symptoms whether the treatment is drug or behavior therapy.

CLOMIPRAMINE AND THE SEROTONIN HYPOTHESIS

One of the promises of neuropharmacology is that drugs can serve not only as treatments but also as neurochemical probes. Unfortunately, we know very little about how drugs work as treatments and only a bit more about how to use them as probes. Clomipramine is an excellent case in point. This drug, relative to other tricyclic antidepressants, is one of the most potent inhibitors of serotonin uptake into neurons. Predictably, its effects on serotonin uptake have been tied to its antiobsessional effects. In support of this "serotonin hypothesis" the following observations can be marshalled. First, in two studies, the improvement in obsessional symptoms correlated positively with plasma levels of clomipramine (Insel et al. 1983a; Stern et al. 1980). Second, decreases in the levels of the serotonin metabolite 5-hydroxyindoleacetic acid (5-HIAA) in cerebrospinal fluid (CSF) correlated significantly with the antiobsessional response to clomipramine

Table 2   Amine Uptake IC_{50} Rat Brain Synaptosomes

	Serotonin (μM)	Norepinephrine (μM)	Dopamine (μM)
Clomipramine	0.018	0.060	7.0*
Desmethylclomipramine	0.12	0.002	5.3
Imipramine	0.14	0.028	24.0
Desmethylimipramine	1.1	0.003	18.0*
Zimelidine	0.13	2.7	12.0
Norzimelidine	0.04	0.076	12.0

Note. All data are taken from Ross and Renyi (1977), except those marked with an asterisk, which are taken from Benfield et al. (1980).

(Asberg et al. 1982). Third, L-tryptophan, a precursor of serotonin (as well as other active amines) has been reported to reduce obsessional symptoms (Yaryura-Tobias et al. 1977). Permitting the logical error of using a correlation of treatment response to develop a theory of cause, one might conclude that obsessional patients have a deficit in serotonergic function, analogous to what has been suggested previously for certain rodent and human models of aggression (Eichelman and Thoa 1973; Brown et al. 1982).

One problem with this hypothesis is that clomipramine is a very complicated drug. It is metabolized in vivo to desmethylclomipramine, a compound with potent effects on norepinephrine uptake. In humans, desmethylclomipramine is present at approximately a two-fold greater concentration than its parent compound (Insel et al. 1983a). Still, in one particular aspect of serotonin uptake—affinity for the imipramine binding site— both clomipramine and desmethylclomipramine are extremely potent (Paul et al. 1981).

To further investigate the importance of serotonin uptake for improvement in obsessional symptoms, we recently compared zimelidine and desipramine, two more neurochemically selective drugs. In Table 2, the relative selectivity of these drugs can be derived from their IC_{50}s, the concentration of drug that produces 50 percent inhibition of amine uptake. In each case, the lower the IC_{50}, the more potent the drug is for uptake blockade.

Zimelidine, a bicyclic antidepressant, is, along with its major metabolite norzimelidine, a relatively selective serotonin uptake blocker (Ross and Renyi 1977). Desmethylimipramine or desipramine, a tricyclic antidepressant, blocks neuronal re-uptake of norepinephrine at very low concentrations but only weakly affects serotonin uptake (Aberg-Wistedt et al. 1981). If the serotonin hypothesis were valid, then zimelidine should reduce obsessional symptoms whereas desipramine should be antidepressant and not antiobsessional.

Preliminary results ($n = 13$) from this comparison suggest that the hypothesis is not valid. Neither zimelidine nor desipramine has been helpful to patients on clinical ratings of obsessionality. These same subjects, when switched over to clomipramine, have shown statistically significant decreases in obsessional symptoms on a global obsessional scale. It is unlikely that this difference in clinical response reflects a difference in serotonin uptake as cerebrospinal fluid 5-HIAA showed very similar reductions following treatment with zimelidine and clomipramine (-47 percent and -45 percent, respectively).

These preliminary findings support the notion that clomipramine is selective as an "antiobsessional" agent among antidepressants. The mechanism of this selectivity is unclear. A role for serotonin, while intriguing, is not supported by our preliminary results with zimelidine. Furthermore, the effects on serotonin uptake are acute while the therapeutic effects take many weeks to develop. Chronic clomipramine administration is associated with a complex profile of effects most of which are shared by other antidepressants. These include the down-regulation of beta-adrenergic receptors as well as effects on the brain serotonergic systems (Charney et al. 1981).

The mechanism of action of clomipramine in obsessive-compulsive disorder may depend on a different neurochemical system altogether. For instance, clomipramine has been reported to potentiate the antinociceptive effects of opiates (Sewell and Lee 1980). Early in this century Janet (1903) noted that opium relieved obsessional symptoms. The opiate antagonist naloxone has recently been reported to exacerbate obsessional doubt (Insel and Pickar 1983). While the evidence is still very preliminary, these fragmentary observations suggest a novel focus for research.

As in so much of neuropharmacology, the question still remains: what neurochemical action is relevant to the clinical effect? At least in this case, where preliminary results suggest that one compound may show some selective clinical advantage the question can be focused to "what makes this tricyclic different from other tricyclics?" The answer to this question may ultimately disclose clues to the neurochemical basis of obsessive-compulsive disorder and symptoms such as doubt, guilt, intrusive thoughts, and ego-dystonic fears.

THE SHORTCOMINGS OF PHARMACOLOGIC TREATMENT

Medication is a treatment, not a cure for obsessive-compulsive disorder. Patients typically report that the symptoms persist but they cause less interference and are resisted more successfully. As a result, patients are able to return to work or school and the increased activities successfully distract from the remaining obsessions or rituals. Occasionally (three of 19 cases in our series), the symptoms may ultimately disappear. Unfortunately, discontinuing the medication even after a year of treatment may precipitate a relapse. In our initial study (Insel et al. 1983a) relapse occurred in nearly every case within three weeks of stopping clomipramine. Asberg and her coworkers (1982) have reported follow-ups after longer medication treatments that were not followed by relapse. At the present time, we do not know how long to continue pharmacologic treatment.

Because drug treatment is likely to be chronic, side effects may pose a major problem. Clomipramine frequently causes lethargy, constipation, sexual dysfunction (anorgasmia), and weight gain. Each of these symptoms may be intolerable to an obsessional patient. Lethargy, in particular, may exacerbate compulsive symptoms as patients feel less capable of resisting rituals.

Occasionally, the act of taking medicine may become a focus for obsessional preoccupation. Elaborate and prolonged rituals of counting and recounting pills with uncertainty about what was ingested may become severe enough to preclude pharmacologic treatment. Patients with obsessional slowness may devote one or two hours each day to unproductive attempts to take medicine.

Finally, it needs to be emphasized that for nearly all obsessive-compulsive disorder patients, pharmacologic management is only one dimension of what must be a multidimensional treatment approach. As the symptoms are likely to be chronic, the context in which they have persisted needs careful attention. Providing a role for the family in the treatment may be critical to ultimate outcome. In addition, these patients are likely to need long term support and directive interventions. Encouraging obsessional patients to take risks and to push themselves into work or school may yield very substantial improvements. Whatever the ultimate etiology of this intriguing disorder, the people who suffer with obsessions and compulsions are usually guilt-ridden and socially isolated. As with any chronic illness, the psychological complications are profound. Pharmacotherapy is not a substitute for psychotherapy. Ideally, both should work together to facilitate change.

CONCLUSION

Pharmacotherapy may be particularly important for obsessionals who cannot be treated successfully with behavioral methods. Clomipramine, which has been the most widely studied drug for obsessive-compulsive disorder, appears more effective than placebo and may be more effective than some other antidepressants. Clomipramine is not yet available in the United States. Although one might assume that the unsubstituted tertiary tricyclic, imipramine, would be the next best compound available, there is currently inadequate evidence of its effectiveness for reducing obsessions in a controlled trial (Mavissakalian and Michelson 1983). Case reports suggest that MAO inhibitors might be helpful, possibly for those patients who do not respond to tricyclics. Other classes of drugs, such as anxiolytics, anticonvulsants, or antipsychotics may prove useful for selective aspects of the obsessive compulsive syndrome, but well designed, controlled trials of these agents have yet to be undertaken.

References

Aberg-Wistedt A, Jostell K-G, Ross SB, et al: Effects of zimelidine and desipramine on serotonin and noradrenaline uptake mechanisms in relation to plasma concentrations and to therapeutic effect during treatment of depression. Psychopharmacology 74:297–305, 1981

Ananth J: Treatment of obsessive compulsive neurosis: pharmacological approach. Psychosomatics 17:180–184, 1976

Ananth J, Solyom L, Bryntwick S, et al: Chlorimipramine therapy for obsessive-compulsive neurosis. Am J Psychiatry 136:700–701, 1979

Ananth J, Pecknold JC, van der Steen N, et al: Double blind comparative study of clomipramine and amitriptyline in obsessive neurosis. Prog Neuropsychopharmacol 5:257–264, 1981

Annesley PT: Nardil response in a chronic obsessive compulsive. Br J Psychiatry 115:748, 1969

Asberg M, Thoren P, Bertilsson L: Clomipramine treatment of obsessive disorder: biochemical and clinical aspects. Psychopharmacol Bull 18:13–21, 1982

Beech HR, Perigault J: Toward a theory of obsessional disorder, in Obsessional States. Edited by Beech HR. London, Methuen, 1974, pp. 113–142

Benfield DP, Harries CM, Luscombe DK: Some pharmacological aspects of desmethylclomipramine. Postgrad Med J 56:13–16, 1980

Black A: The natural history of obsessional neurosis, in Obsessional States. Edited by Beech HR. London, Methuen, 1974

Brown GL, Ebert MH, Goyer PF, et al: Aggression, suicide, and serotonin: relationship to CSF amine metabolites. Am J Psychiatry 139:741–746, 1982

Capstick N: Clinical experience in the treatment of obsessional states. J Int Med Res 5 (Suppl 5):71–80, 1977

Charney DS, Menkes DB, Heninger GR: Receptor sensitivity and the mechanism of action of antidepressant treatment. Arch Gen Psychiatry 38:1160–1180, 1981

Coryell W: Obsessive compulsive disorder and primary unipolar depression. J Nerv Ment Dis 169:220–224, 1981

Cottraux JA, Bouvard M, Claustrat B, et al: Abnormal dexamethasone suppression test in primary obsessive compulsive patients: a confirmatory report. Psychiatry Res (in press)

Eichelman B, Thoa NB: The aggressive monoamines. Biol Psychiatry 6:143–156, 1973

Foa EB: Failure in treating obsessive-compulsives. Behav Res Ther 17:169–176, 1979

Gittleson N: The fate of obsessions in depressive psychosis. Br J Psychiatry 112:705–708, 1966

Goodwin D, Guze S, Robins E: Follow-up studies in obsessional neurosis. Arch Gen Psychiatry 20:182–187, 1969

Insel TR: Obsessive compulsive disorder: five clinical questions and a suggested approach. Compr Psychiatry 23:241–248, 1982

Insel TR, Alterman I, Murphy DL: Antiobsessional and antidepressant effects with clomipramine. Psychopharmacol Bull 18:315–319, 1982a

Insel TR, Gillin JC, Moore A, et al: Sleep in obsessive-compulsive disorder. Arch Gen Psychiatry 39:1372–1377, 1982b

Insel TR, Kalin NH, Guttmacher LB, et al: The dexamethasone suppression test in patients with primary obsessive-compulsive disorder. Psychiatry Res 6:153–158, 1982c

Insel TR, Pickar D: Naloxone administration in obsessive compulsive disorder: a report of two cases. Am J Psychiatry 140:1219–1220, 1983

Insel TR, Murphy DL, Cohen RM, et al: Obsessive-compulsive disorder: a double-blind trial of clomipramine and clorgyline. Arch Gen Psychiatry 40:605–612, 1983a

Insel TR, Hoover C, Murphy DL: The parents of patients with obsessive compulsive disorder. Psychol Med 13:807–811, 1983b

Isberg R: A comparison of Phenelzine and imipramine in an obsessive-compulsive patient. Am J Psychiatry 138:1250–1251, 1981

Jain VK, Swinson RP, Thomas JE: Phenelzine in obsessional neurosis Br J Psychiatry 117:237–238, 1970

Janet P: Les Obsessions et la Psychasthenie. Paris, Bailliere, 1903

Jenike MA: Rapid response of severe obsessive-compulsive disorder to tranylcypromine. Am J Psychiatry 138:1249–1250, 1981

Jenike MA, Surman OS, Cassem NH, et al: Monoamine oxidase inhibitors in obsessive-compulsive disorder. J Clin Psychiatry 4:131–132, 1983

Knesevich JW: Successful treatment of obsessive compulsive disorder with clonidine hydrochloride. Am J Psychiatry 139:364–365, 1982

Lopez-Ibor JJ: Intravenous perfusions of monochlorimipramine: technique and results, in Proceedings of the Sixth International Congress of the CINP. Amsterdam, Excerpta Medica Foundation, 1969, pp 519–521

Marks IM: Are there anticompulsive or antiphobic drugs? Review of the evidence. Br J Psychiatry 143:338–347, 1983

Marks IM, Stern R, Mawson D, et al: Clomipramine and exposure for obsessive compulsive rituals. Br J Psychiatry 136:1–25, 1980

Maudsley H: The Pathology of the Mind. London, Macmillan, 1895

Mavissakalian M, Michelson L: Tricyclic antidepressants in obsessive compulsive disorder: antiobsessional or antidepressant agents? J Nerv Ment Dis 171:301–306, 1983

Mayer-Gross W, Slater E, Roth M: Clinical Psychiatry. London, Cassell, 1960

Montgomery SA: Clomipramine in obsessional neurosis: a placebo controlled trial. Pharmaceutical Medicine 1:189–192, 1980

Orvin G: Treatment of the phobic obsessive compulsive patient with oxazepam. Psychosomatics 8:278–280, 1967

Paul SM, Rehavi M, Hulihan B, et al: A rapid and sensitive radioreceptor assay for tertiary amine tricyclic antidepressants. Communications in Psychopharmacology 4:487–494, 1981

Rack PH: Clinical experience in the treatment of obsessional states. J Int Med Res 5(Suppl 5):81–96, 1977

Rao AV: A controlled trial with Valium in obsessive compulsive state. J Indian Med Assoc 42:564–567, 1964

Ross SB, Renyi AL: Inhibition of the neuronal uptake of 5-hydroxytryptamine and noradrenaline in rat brain by (Z)- and (E)-3-(4-bromophenyl)-N, N-dimethyl-3-(3-pyridyl) allylamines and their secondary analogues. Neuropharmacology 16:57–63, 1977

Sewell RDE, Lee RL: Opiate receptors, endorphins, and drug therapy. Postgrad Med J 56(Suppl 1):25–30, 1980

Siever L, Insel TR, Jimerson D, et al: Blunted growth hormone response to clonidine in obsessive-compulsive patients. Br J Psychiatry 142:184–188, 1983

Stern RS, Marks IM, Mawson D, et al: Clomipramine and exposure for compulsive rituals: plasma levels, side effects, and outcome. Br J Psychiatry 136:161–166, 1980

Stern TA, Jenike MA: Treatment of obsessive-compulsive disorder with lithium carbonate. Psychosomatics 24:671–673, 1983

Thoren P, Asberg M, Cronholm B, et al: Clomipramine treatment of obsessive compulsive disorder: a controlled clinical trial. Arch Gen Psychiatry 37:1281–1289, 1980

Welner A, Reich T, Robins E, et al: Obsessive-compulsive neurosis: record, follow-up, and family studies. Compr Psychiatry 17:527–539, 1976

Yaryura-Tobias JA, Bhagavan HN: l-Tryptophan in obsessive compulsive disorders. Am J Psychiatry 134:1298–1299, 1977

Zahn T, Insel TR, Murphy DL: Psychophysiologic changes during pharmacologic treatment of obsessive compulsive disorder. Br J Psychiatry (in press)

5

Obsessive-Compulsive Disorder: Cognitive Approaches in Context

Jean A. Hamilton, M.D.
Sheryle W. Alagna, Ph.D.

5

Obsessive-Compulsive Disorder: Cognitive Approaches in Context

Beck (1983) has commented on the tendency for investigators of psychopathology to adopt an overly simplistic, either-or approach to diagnosis. For example, a "thought" disorder has long been considered a diagnostic feature of schizophrenia; in contrast, depression and anxiety have been regarded as primarily "affective" disorders (Beck 1976). Of course these categories are not held to be mutually exclusive in actual practice, since most clinicians recognize "flat affect" (American Psychiatric Association 1980) and even depression (deVries 1983) in schizophrenia, as well as memory (Silberman et al. 1983; Weingartner et al. 1981) and other cognitive complaints or disturbances in depression.

Obsessive-compulsive disorder is currently classified as an anxiety disorder (American Psychiatric Association 1980). Along with other anxiety disorders (Leckman et al. 1983), however, obsessionality shares certain clinical features with depression (Insel 1982). Because of the historical tendency to view depression and anxiety as primarily "affective" or emotional disorders, cognitive approaches to obsessive-compulsive disorder have been relatively neglected in recent discussions of evaluation and treatment. That recurrent thought intrusions are characteristic of obsessive-compulsive disorder, however, reminds us of the need to examine concomitant cognitive processes. A cognitive approach to obsessive-compulsive disorder requires both a comprehensive, theoretical perspective and an adequate assessment paradigm. In this chapter, we describe cognitive features of obsessionality in the context of ongoing symptoms and affect, demonstrate a new cognitive approach to clinical evaluations, and outline strategies for treatment.

COGNITIVE AND AFFECTIVE FEATURES IN OBSESSIVE-COMPULSIVE DISORDER: BEYOND THE EITHER-OR APPROACH

Features of Thought Disorders

Beck (1976) has described various "emotional disorders" in terms of their characteristic thought content, primary rules, and other cognitive features. Based on our clinical research experience with this patient group, we have extrapolated from Beck's cognitive approach to depression, anxiety neurosis, and phobias (with mention of obsessive-compulsive disorder) and developed a cognitive approach to obsessive-compulsive disorder, as summarized in Table 1.

Content. The defining thought content we propose for obsessive-compulsive disorder was derived directly from Beck's description of phobias; the obsessive is primarily concerned with the risk of imminent danger, but is also focused on doubt and warnings (obsessions), or the need to perform a specific act to ward off danger (compulsions). That is, obsessives go one step beyond phobics and build into their thought content what to do about the feared situation.

Rules. Typical obsessive rules might be as follows. First, "If I do X (a specific thought, image, or action), then I will be able to cope with a dangerous situation." This contrasts with the phobic who mainly seeks to *avoid* the danger. A corollary is that: "Otherwise, I will not only be out of control, but will also be dangerous to others; therefore, others are at risk and should avoid me." These cognitive rules are often associated with a grandiosity

Table 1 Cognitive Features of Obsessive-Compulsive Disorder

Content	Rules	Other Cognitive Features and Examples	Examples of Cognitive Features That May be Shared Across the "Emotional" Disorders
Imminent risk of danger	If I do X (a specific thought or action), then I will be able to cope with a dangerous situation	Stereotyped thought intrusions Under-inclusiveness (on "Essential category" tests)	*Distortions and Maladaptive Thoughts* Polarized, dichotomous thinking Rigidity and perfectionism Overgeneralization and arbitrary inference
with focus on doubt or the need for specific thoughts, images or actions to ward off danger	Otherwise, I am out of control	Doubt and indecision	Impaired concentration or memory complaints
	But others are at risk and should avoid me, lest I contaminate them also	*Shared Primarily with Phobias:*	
	And I can also never get help or ever get well The risks of danger are imminent *Example of a Rule That May Be Shared Across Beck's Emotional Disorders:*	Overevaluation Dysfunctional estimation of risks *Shared Primarily Across Anxiety Disorders:*	
	I am responsible for everything (when anything goes wrong it is my fault).	Tendency to assume negative valence and to "catastrophize," and to anticipate losing control	

that reaches delusional proportions. For example, one woman repeatedly voiced the concern that her hand washing would "drain the local reservoir."

A related cognitive "rule" is that: "I can never get well" (since the risk—contamination, for example—is ubiquitous), with the corollary that "no one can help me; and if they try, they will be as contaminated or otherwise harmed as I am."

One might even think of the obsessives' pervasive and exaggerated estimation of "risks" as reflecting an underlying cognitive rule. On Steiner's (1972) measure of risk-taking, obsessional patients scored low; as pointed out by Salzman (1980) the obsessional demand for continual reassurance is antithetical to risk-taking. And Carr (1974) has recognized that the obsessives' characteristic sense of doubt and indecision may be related to their rules for processing information about risk and harm. Card-sorting and other tasks, for example, have corroborated the clinical impression that obsessives show increased requirements for information before they take the risk of making a decision (Beech 1974; Milner et al. 1971).

And finally, there is the rule that: "I am responsible for everything"; or "when something goes wrong, it is my fault," which is primarily shared with depression. In particular, the obsessive will likely focus on the enormous and ever-present responsibility to protect others from harmful contamination or some other feared, catastrophic event.

Other Features.   Certain cognitive features are relatively characteristic of obsessive-compulsive disorder. Obsessive-compulsive disorder is characterized by recurrent cognitions that intrude on the obsessives' stream of consciousness. Despite effortful resistance, obsessives find their attention rigidly focused on a narrowed range of experience. From this cognitive perspective, obsessive-compulsive disorder approaches one of the key features of schizophrenia (see Chapter 1).

Although schizophrenia and obsessive-compulsive disorder are both characterized by intrusive thoughts and images, Reed (1969) suggested that their thinking could also be contrasted. In studies of

Table 2 Comparison of Cognitive Features by Diagnostic Group

Cognitive Feature	Obsessive-Compulsive Disorder	Schizophrenia
Category definition	Under-inclusive	Over-inclusive
Associations	Fixed	Loose
Resistance	Effortful	(Absent)

category definition, assessed by asking subjects to underline only the essential words that define another word, schizophrenics typically underline too many, nonessential words; whereas, obsessives underline too few essential words. Thus, on this cognitive dimension, schizophrenics can be characterized as "over-inclusive," and obsessives as "under-inclusive." Confirmation of Reed's approach (1977) with obsessives comes from the work of Persons and Foa (in press); in a card-sorting test of category definition, obsessives used more piles with fewer items per category, which is thought to suggest overly "complex concepts" and narrow, or under-inclusive thinking.

Schizophrenics also exhibit "loose associations," which contrast sharply with the rigid, more stereotyped associations of obsessives. Moreover, obsessives resist their recurrent thought intrusions, while such effortful resistance is not a defining feature of schizophrenia. These tentative comparisons are summarized in Table 2.

Shared primarily with phobias or anxiety neurosis are (1) over-evaluation, where certain concerns like dust on a spoon take on exaggerated importance, a tendency confirmed in studies by Walker (1967) (also see Beech 1974, pp. 150–151), and (2) "catastrophizing," where the worst possible outcome is typically anticipated. An example of these features is that one obsessive-compulsive patient felt that "having lice" would be absolutely "catastrophic," whereas her continual day-to-day fear was literally of louse-ing up.

Moreover, a variety of thought distortions and maladaptive thoughts that Beck has described in great detail for depressives are common among obsessive-compulsive patients. Examples are as follows:

1. Polarized, dichotomous thinking (one patient talked of people as being either "O.K." and "clean like us," or else being "filthy"; i.e., contaminated or uncontaminated);

2. Rigidity and perfectionism (where obsessive-compulsive patients reject themselves and others because of impossibly high standards such as perfect rituals or total cleanliness), and
3. Overgeneralization and arbitrary inference (where obsessive-compulsive patients, like depressives, may believe that they are either totally accepted or else rejected).

Features of Affective Disorders

Elsewhere in this monograph (Chapter 4), the complex relationship of obsessive-compulsive disorder to depression is discussed. Briefly, the two disorders share certain clinical and biological features, and at least 50 percent of most obsessive-compulsive disorder samples are complicated by secondary depressions. For instance, dysphoria, indecision, and doubt are common to both syndromes, blurring the distinction between obsessional and affective disorder.

METHODS OF ASSESSING COGNITION IN OBSESSIVE-COMPULSIVE DISORDER

Traditional Baseline Measures

Neuropsychological testing has been useful in characterizing a variety of psychiatric disorders. As discussed in another chapter, several neurological findings have suggested a cognitive or neuropsychological impairment in obsessionality.

Yet attempts to characterize obsessive-compulsive disorder with neurological measures like the electroencephalogram or with batteries of neuropsychological tests have met with mixed results at best (Insel et al. 1983b). In addition, when obsessive-compulsive patients were compared to age-sex matched controls on brain Evoked Response measures (Insel et al. 1982), we found several significant differences, although these do not in themselves characterize a neuropsychological syndrome. Hence, traditional approaches to neuropsychological assessment using one-time, baseline measures have not yielded consistent findings in obsessive-compulsive disorder.

The Use of Amphetamine in a Provocative Testing Paradigm

Given this description of cognitive features in obsessive-compulsive disorder, we wondered whether changes in obsessional symptoms might co-vary with changes along a cognitive dimension. For example, we hypothesized that attention or sustained vigilance—aspects of cognition that can be objectively measured—might vary directly with the intensity of intrusive thoughts. To test this hypothesis, we administered a single dose of d-amphetamine, a drug known to alter attentional performance in nonpatient volunteers (Buchsbaum et al. 1981), to patients with obsessive-compulsive disorder. We evaluated both improvement in obsessions and in attentional performance, and we correlated changes in obsessional symptoms with changes in attention.

In a double-blind, placebo-controlled design that is described elsewhere in detail (Insel et al. 1983a), we administered 30 mg d-amphetamine (free base) to 12 DSM-III diagnosed obsessive-compulsive patients. We used the continuous performance test (CPT) as a measure of sustained attention. This is a test that requires the subject to push a button when a target sequence of letters appears among a sequence of randomized letters. We also used smooth pursuit eye-tracking as a separate index of attention that is thought to be automatized, or less voluntary (Holzman et al. 1978). Thus, our design allowed us to examine the process of change in the interrelationships between cognition, affect, and symptomatology in obsessive-compulsive disorder.

In the first three hours following amphetamine administration, we observed a significant decrease in clinically rated obsessional symptoms that averaged 23 percent. This improvement in obsessional symptoms was significantly correlated with improved performance on the CPT ($r = 0.62$, $p < 0.05$). Decreases in obsessionality were consistent across the sample even though clinically rated changes in mood revealed that some patients became more dysphoric while others became activated. Hence, the results indicated independent effects of amphetamine on mood and obsessions. More importantly, they suggested a dissociation between amphetamine effects on mood and attention that allowed us to tease apart the specific relationship between obsessional change and attentional performance in a defined emotional context. Thus, it appears that obsessional symptoms are more closely related to attentional processes than to affect per se.

Along with improved attention, we found that there was a subjective sense of better concentration and of fewer distractions. Some patients reported a diminished intensity of symptoms or an enchanced ability to resist their obsessions. As one patient reported: "[I] still have the thoughts, but they don't bother me as much. . . . [I] still see specks on me but I can live with it. [Now I] can cope with these obsessions better and throw it off; [I] don't have to try to correct it. . . . "

Also, we found that subjects with the poorest eye-tracking off-drug showed the most CPT improvement on amphetamine (Siever et al., manuscript in preparation). Thus, the poorest eye-trackers were not more disorganized by amphetamine; rather they evidenced amphetamine-induced improvement in voluntary attention. Perhaps this freedom of attention is related to their subjective sense of "throwing off" or of better resisting the obsessions.

In summary, we found the amphetamine challenge to be a useful assessment paradigm for examining the association of obsessionality to cognitive, attentional measures. Since the dissociation of attention from mood was not apparent from baseline measures, we believe that provocative tests, using repeated measures to assess the actual process of change, may be a better paradigm for clinical evaluations.

Further analysis of our data is planned to examine the actual time-course of cognitive attentional changes versus those occurring in obsessionality and mood. A preliminary look at this data, however, reveals that the attentional (CPT) improvement precedes the obsessional improvement, a finding that lends further support to Meldman's (1970) hypothesis that attention may be a critical dimension in obsessive-compulsive disorder. Moreover, a very early look at our data on memory functioning on amphetamine vs. placebo in this group suggests the pertinence of certain models of remembering in obsessionality, as suggested by Persons and Foa (in press), although these effects were more pronounced for the females as a group. Future studies may also clarify whether the amphetamine challenge has a role in clinical and diagnostic evaluations of obsessive-compulsive disorder.

IMPLICATIONS OF A CONTEXTUAL COGNITIVE APPROACH FOR TREATMENT STRATEGIES

Cognitive therapy is generally directed at correcting faulty premises and beliefs or altering thinking habits via self-monitoring techniques, discussion, or by the rehearsal of new thinking habits. At a recent conference, Foa and Kozak (1983) summarized cognitive as well as behavioral treatment for anxiety disorders including obsessive-compulsive disorder. All "cognitive" techniques they examined actually included an exposure component for treating anxiety. Since cognitive-behavioral techniques overlap, the reader is referred to Foa's work on exposure and response prevention in obsessive-compulsive disorder (Chapter 3). Overall, however, the existing studies of cognitive techniques with obsessive-compulsive disorder have not been encouraging. In one study of 15 obsessive-compulsive patients, for example, Emmelkamp et al. (1980) found that cognitive techniques did not enhance the efficacy of exposure techniques.

On the other hand, Foa and Kozak (1983) have suggested that more precise elaboration and application of cognitive approaches may prove helpful. With obsessionality, for example, there may be an impairment in the very rules for processing certain emotional information, and the processing may vary according to exposure to feared stimuli (Persons and Foa, in press). For instance, the obsessive may exaggerate risks according to the "rule" that danger is imminent. This suggests that it may be important to reeducate obsessives to reappraise situations more realistically. The process of reeducation would be directed at the ways in which they draw catastrophic, over-generalized causal inferences from arbitrary, overvalued events. For example, exposure exercises might combine repeated estimates of the risk of harm or the consequences of a mistake, along with reports of the anxiety level accompanying a feared event.

Another approach, suggested by Salzman (1980) involves the cautious encouragement of risk-taking in obsessive-compulsive disorder patients. Although the estimation of risk is certainly an issue for these patients, their self-reports and actual risk-taking behavior may vary. For example, we found a mixed pattern of scores on Zuckerman's self-report measure of Sensation Seeking (Zuckerman and Neeb 1979) in our group of obsessive-compulsive disorder patients. Although one compulsive "checker" obtained a very high score, this patient apparently guarded against the fantasized recklessness and feared losing control. Given this interpretation, the initial therapeutic intervention was directed at her exaggerated cognitions about risk-taking, which she apparently equated with helplessness through a chain of unstated inferences, and cautious encouragement of risk-taking came later.

To the extent that the symptomatic obsessives' attentional focus is outside of volitional control, it is not surprising that the obsessive has a pervasive sense of doubt, indecision, and fears about harm and risk-taking, as may be reflected in excessive "checking." Regardless of whether or not there is an underlying neuropsychological deficit contributing to this attentional constriction, cognitive techniques may help obsessives to unlearn the old rules and to learn more appropriate rules for processing certain information. That is, self-management techniques can be directed at both correcting primary psychopathological processes and at strengthening secondary, compensatory processes that may have developed as a result of neuropsychological deficits.

DISCUSSION

Like other anxiety disorders, obsessionality shares certain features both with "thought" and with "affective" disorders. Having recognized the problem with dichotomous conceptual models, we explored cognitive approaches to obsessionality in the context of ongoing emotional and symptomatic states. The link between obsessionality and attentional functioning was revealed only by a provocative testing procedure, with the concurrent assessment of cognitive, affective, and symptomatic changes and their covariation.

As an eminently "mixed" disorder, obsessionality may emerge as a critical example that will help focus clinical and research attention on the inherent interrelationships between cognition and affect, particularly as these linkages vary across biologically and situationally defined contexts (Hamilton 1981; Hamilton, in press). Although obsessionality has proven relatively resistant to traditional psychodynamic or verbal insight-oriented therapies, a better understanding of cognitive processing in this disorder may aid in the development of clinically useful evaluation paradigms, and more effective cognitive-behavioral techniques.

References

American Psychiatric Association: Diagnostic and Statistical Manual of Mental Disorders, 3rd ed. Washington, DC, American Psychiatric Association, 1980

Beck AT: Cognitive Therapy and the Emotional Disorders. New York, International Universities Press, 1976

Beck AT: Cognitive therapy of depression; in New Perspectives in Treatment of Depression: Old Controversies and New Approaches. Edited by Clayton PJ, Barret JE. New York, Raven Press, 1983

Beech H: Obsessional States. London, Methuen, 1974

Buchsbaum MS, Coppola R, Gershon ES, et al: Evoked potential measures of attention and psychopathology. Advances in Biological Psychiatry 6:186–194, 1981

Carr A: Compulsive neurosis: a review of the literature. Psychol Bull 81:311–318, 1974

deVries M: Temporal patterning in psychiatric symptoms. Paper presented at the World Congress of Psychiatry, Vienna, July 1983

Emmelkamp PMG, van de Helm H, van Zanten B, et al: Contributions of self-instructional training to the effectiveness of exposure in vivo: a comparison with obsessive-compulsive patients. Behav Res Ther 18:61–66, 1980

Foa EB, Kozak MJ: Treatment of anxiety disorders: implications for psychopathology. Paper presented at the National Institute of Mental Health Conference on Anxiety and Anxiety Disorders, Tuxedo, NY, September 1983

Hamilton, JA: Attention, personality, and the self-regulation of mood: absorbing interest and boredom, in Progress in Experimental Personality Research, Vol. 10. Edited by Maher BA. New York, Academic Press, 1981

Hamilton JA: The development of interest and enjoyment. Journal of Youth and Adolescence (in press)

Holzman PS, Levy DL, Proctor LR: The several qualities of attention in schizophrenia. J Psychiatr Res 14:99–110, 1978

Insel TR: Obsessive compulsive disorder: five clinical questions and a suggested approach. Compr Psychiatry 23:241–251, 1982

Insel TR, Alterman IS, Cohen RM, et al: Psychobiological studies of obsessional disorder. Paper presented at the 135th Annual Meeting of the American Psychiatric Association, Toronto, Canada, May 1982

Insel TR, Hamilton, JA, Guttmacher LB, et al: D-amphetamine in obsessive-compulsive disorder. Psychopharmacology 80:231–235, 1983a

Insel TR, Donnelly EF, Lalakea ML, et al: Neurological and neuropsychological studies of patients with obsessive-compulsive disorder. Biol Psychiatry 18:741–751, 1983b

Leckman J, Weissman M, Merikanges KR, et al: Panic disorder and major depression. Arch Gen Psychiatry 40:1055–1060, 1983

Meldman MJ: Diseases of Attention and Perception. New York, Pergamon, 1970

Milner AD, Beech HR, Walker V: Decision processes and obsessional behavior. British Journal of Social and Clinical Psychology 10:88–89, 1971

Persons JB, Foa EB: Thinking processes in obsessive-compulsive disorder. Behav Res Ther (in press)

Reed GF: "Under-inclusion"—a characteristic of obsessional personality disorder. Br J Psychiatry 115:781–785, 1969

Reed G: Obsessional personality disorder and remembering. Br J Psychiatry 130:177–183, 1977

Salzman L: The Treatment of Obsessive Compulsive Personality. New York, Jason Aronson, 1980

Siever LJ, Hamilton JA, Insel TR, et al: Smooth pursuit eye tracking: effects of amphetamine in obsessive-compulsives. Manuscript in preparation

Silberman EK, Weingartner H, Post RM: Thinking disorder in depression. Arch Gen Psychiatry 40:775–780, 1983

Steiner J: A questionnaire study of risk-taking psychiatric patients. Br J Med Psychol 45:365–374, 1972

Walker VJ: An investigation of ritualistic behavior in obsessional patients. Unpublished Ph.D. thesis, Institute of Psychiatry, University of London, 1967

Weingartner H, Cohen RM, Murphy DL, et al: Cognitive processes in depression. Arch Gen Psychiatry 38:42–47, 1981

Zuckerman M, Neeb M: Sensation seeking and psychopathology. J Psychiatr Res 1:225–264, 1979

6

The Dynamics of Obsessive-Compulsive Disorder

Robert D. Coursey, Ph.D.

6

The Dynamics of Obsessive-Compulsive Disorder

The patient with obsessive-compulsive disorder repeatedly feels compelled to attend to or engage in thoughts, fantasies, or behaviors that are repugnant, frightening, distressful, and reprehensible. Even a superficial exposure to the inner experience of obsessive-compulsive disorder leads immediately to two questions.

The first question is why there is this pressure to be preoccupied with punishing internal experiences or bizarre behavior. While early theories (see Salzman and Thaler [1981] for a brief review of history and theories) included possession by demonic forces, Freud emphasized a secularized, psychological version of this: the internal pressure from preoedipal, anal-sadistic impulses. Many later theorists such as Sandor Rado emphasized repressed rage, unacceptable hostile or sexual impulses. However, another early theorist, Janet, focused on a complementary aspect, not the heightened impulse but the weakened controls, the psychic fatigue and lack of energy to control one's thoughts and actions.

The second question is how these patients deal with their regressive, anal-sadistic impulses. Three main coping mechanisms have been described. First, Freud and later theorists have focused on certain defenses such as isolation, displacement, reaction formation, and undoing. Second, most current theorists, including behaviorally oriented researchers, would see the compulsive behavior as secondary to the internal states, either as a way of controlling or relieving the anxiety and other inner feelings. Third, starting with Freud, most psychodynamic theorists also postulate that obsessive thoughts or fantasies (however horrible) are also a defense that distracts or controls the person from recognizing an even more terrible aspect of themselves. While this may be true in some cases, e.g., obsessions such as magical sentences, it is also equally plausible that many obsessions may be simply the controlled expression of what the client knows but dislikes—the strong sadistic or sexual impulses that early theorists thought unconscious. From this perspective, the underlying thought or impulse need not be more terrible and different, but merely elaborations and extensions of what the client already experiences and attempts to control within himself. Even those obsessions that clearly seem secondary to the inner impulse are often indirect but conscious acknowledgment of these impulses by the patient, for they are worries about preventing, releasing, or having acted upon the terrible impulse.

Our experience with the assessment of these patients has led us to the following thesis: obsessive-compulsive disorder patients, as opposed to patients with compulsive characters only, are generally aware of primitive instinctual material, particularly aggression. While they do not approve of it, they do acknowledge its presence in their consciousness. With respect to the presence of primary process in their awareness, they are similar to schizophrenic patients. However, they differ from schizophrenics in that they maintain relatively accurate reality testing. The awareness of this unacceptable primary process material leads to massive inhibition, to linguistic, defensive, and behavioral neutralization strategies, and to intense anxiety, guilt, and fears of expression of these impulses.

METHOD OF THE STUDY

The current study was undertaken to document particular aspects of the internal experience of severely obsessional patients. We administered the Rorschach Inkblot test to evaluate instinctual

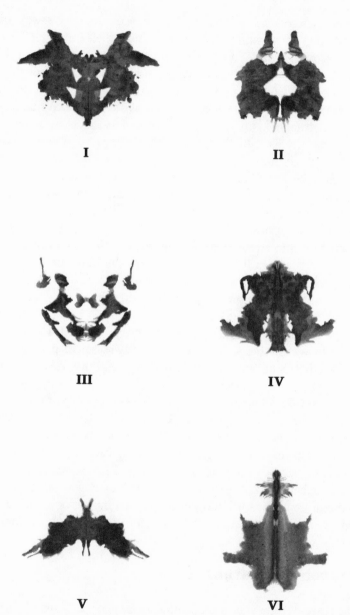

Figure 1 Rorschach inkblots used to test instinctual content and defenses. Cards I, IV, V, VI, and VII are all black; cards II and III also contain red; and cards VIII, IX, and X are all colored.

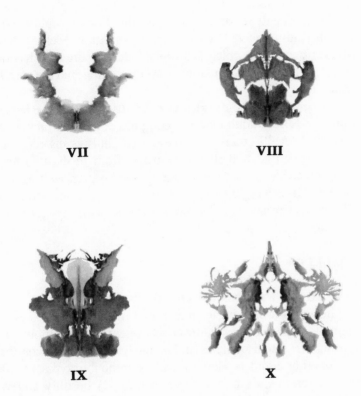

VII   VIII

IX   X

content and defenses. Very little has been written about the
Rorschach and obsessive-compulsive disorders (Schafer 1948,
1954). What does exist has been based on general psychodynamic
theory and single cases, and confuses the compulsive personality
with obsessive-compulsive disorder. While the characteristics discussed in this chapter have all been scored by a wide variety of
Rorschach scales (Exner 1974; Goldfried et al. 1971; Holt 1970), for
clarity and ease of presentation, I will illustrate the findings
primarily by using the patients' actual verbal responses to the
inkblots. Black and white reproductions of the blots are given in
Figure 1.

To examine these patients' general inhibition of impulsive life, we also administered Zuckerman's Sensation Seeking Scale (Zuckerman 1979) which is an excellent measure of behavioral and other forms of disinhibition, novelty seeking, and the need for invariance.

The subjects for these studies were 15 patients (9 male, 6 female) from the NIMH adult obsessive-compulsive disorder project. All met the DSM-III criteria for obsessive-compulsive disorder, nine were hospitalized, and all had been free from medication for at least four weeks at the time of assessment. Ages ranged from 18 to 57, with a mean of 30.7 years. Seven had onset during adulthood. The average duration of illness was 6.5 years, with a range of 1.5 to 13 years.

RESULTS

Primary Process on the Rorschach

The amount of explicit, undisguised material these obsessive-compulsive patients gave more closely resembled the amount and type found on schizophrenic and manic Rorschach protocols than that of other disorders. Here we will examine four types, in order of their prevalence among the responses: (1) hostility and violence, (2) orality and dependency, (3) genital and anal material, and (4) formal thought impairment such as autistic logic.

Hostility and Violence. It is rare to have any explicit hostility on the Rorschach, but here we find explicitly aggressive responses on 60 percent of the protocols. If we score mild or symbolically hostile responses, 80 percent of the patients give such responses. The mean Elizur Hostility score for all patients was 3.8 versus 1.3 among normals (Goldfried et al. 1971). Using Holt's scoring system (Holt 1970) the obsessive-compulsive patients showed aggression on 18 percent of all of their responses to the inkblots. Examples would include card II: "The title of this is The War, because everything looks like fighting, blood. One half is the U.S.; one half is Russia, and the nuclear bomb has been dropped. That's why blood has been splattered. Like the apocalypse." Another example is from card III: "A falcon took a bite out of its prey; a piece of meat is still in its mouth." A last example is from card IX: "Seems like an infant before it's born, still in the womb; seems like in an embryonic sack. It reminds me of blood. It doesn't have skin like we do. A relatively big head; awfully thin neck; and that worries me. Like could kill it easily by squeezing there. Could cut it off." These typical responses contrasted markedly with the socially timid, inhibited, and fearful demeanor and behavior of these patients.

Orality and Dependency. Except among children, oral-dependent responses such as mouth, food, touching, and oral aggressive responses are not common. Yet among our obsessive compulsives, two-thirds of the patients gave mouth and food responses, over one-third of the patients gave baby-dependency type responses, and one-third of the patients touching-holding responses. Examples include this oral-aggressive response from card I: "A bat, looks like its about to prey on something innocent, with its fangs, claws sticking out." A response on card III illustrates the baby-dependency type of response: "Two babies—as if the umbilical cord is still there, still attached. Just looks like they're in limbo." This food response is from card X: "Reminds me of a wishbone. Like my mommy used to say, wishbones."

Genital and Anal Responses Surprisingly for this generally inhibited group, a third of the patients gave genital and anal content for more than 10 percent of their responses. The following response was given to card IV: "Something with big feet looking at me. And on reflection, I don't know what the thing along the middle is, between his feet. First three thoughts, just wondering, don't think it looks like it—either dick, turd, or a stool—something to sit on." Several examples from card VI are "This part reminds me of a rectum of an animal, anus of an animal." (Examiner asks what about the card makes it look like that.) "Just the shape and that it's the opposite end of the cat." Another patient responded to card VI: "First thing I thought about . . . hard to say, ah . . . embarrassed to say it . . . it looks like a man's penis inside a woman." While normal adults occasionally give sexual responses, generally sex organs are briefly named, and the responses do not include the type of slang and unintended pun seen in the first responses, the autistic logic of the second, or sexual activity noted on the third.

Formal Thought Impairment.   Although these patients were screened for schizophrenia, about 20 percent had some formal thinking impairment of a variety of types. These are rarely seen on the Rorschachs of normal adults. One patient gave the following response to card VIII, which I have condensed slightly:

> Top part looks like it could resemble some type of face—imaginary or sinister. Looks like he's rather omnipotent, omniscience.... It destroys the usual theory that something good is over all. Or at least disputes the theory that the supreme being is a good caliber type of person. Possibly its the devil. Or if don't want to look at religious viewpoint, hardship and evil override pleasure. Looks like the sea is cracking; land has a fault in it. It is destroying itself.

One patient gave a brief response to card VI: "Face on it." (Examiner asks, "It?") "The penis." (The penis was a response given earlier.) And on a twist to the proverbial butterfly given to card V, one patient added "The tips of the wings look like alligator heads.... The butterfly wings make me feel shitty—to think an alligator head attached, doesn't jive."

What is clear from all of the primary process type of responses described above is that this impulsive primitive material is not repressed, is readily and consciously available to the patient, and sometimes even forms the basis of their obsessive thoughts. Moreover, this material is not due to prior psychotherapy experiences since few previously had much contact with therapy and fewer still with psychoanalytically oriented therapy.

The Control and Neutralization of Affect

In order to control and neutralize the primitive material that has erupted into consciousness, these obsessive-compulsive patients displayed a variety of responses. Some of these patients expressed the *everyday reactions* of embarrassment, guilt (about a third of the patients), and apologies (about 60 percent of the patients apologized for, or deprecated their performance in some way). About half of the patients used *classical defenses* such as undoing and denial. These defense mechanisms were usually seen across responses, balancing the impulse with its opposite. For instance, one patient first saw "piercing mean eyes peering at me through the dark," then next saw "some type of face smiling, a cartoon figure." A very similar balancing mechanism was frequently seen where hostile and sexual responses were followed with neutral ones, rather than with the opposite affective responses as in the above example. Thus "meat cleaver" was followed by a "necklace," a "mean gorilla" was followed by a "thermometer," and a "man's sex organ, with the shape sticking up" was followed by "can also be construed as a thumb." Twenty percent of the subjects demonstrated denial that failed. They first denied any response, then revealed a sexual or hostile one. For instance, one patient first said that the "red at the bottom means nothing" and the next response was a nuclear war where the red "signifies blood has been splattered." Of course, we do not know what percent of the patients used denial successfully so that their primitive emotional material was inhibited.

But the most widespread way these patients controlled their affect was *through language*, mostly through the choice of emotionally flat, neutral words. About two-thirds of the patients used this form of cold factual language, rather than emotionally hot words. Five different aspects of this language management were observed.

Neutralized Content.   Some patients appeared to neutralize their primitive material by the use of emotionally flat words. While the objects seen are common every day ones, they are extremely unusual choices for the Rorschach (Exner 1974). Examples include responses such as "handles," "footprint," "hand whistle," "walking stick," "metal wash tub," "towel," "hairpiece," etc.

Precise Intellectualized Content.   A second method of neutralizing content is the linguistic side of intellectualization, the use of precise descriptions, little known or technical words and information. Examples include "the Western coast of Alaska," "knife . . . should have said a serrated knife," "tapir," "Sri Lanka," "it's a crab because of ovular body with appendages."

Use of Alternatives.   The need for precision and balance evidently is a more generalized response set, and extended into balancing two affectively neutral responses. Examples of this would be "sort of camels, or a horse on a merry-go-round if not a camel"; "a bowl or a dish or a container"; "maybe a stream down a mountain into a forest, or if not a stream, then a road running through the forest." A more behavioral form of this occurs when the patient repeatedly pointed out the symmetry of the inkblot, or the same response on both sides of the card.

Perseveration.   Occasionally, a patient would find a relatively neutral response such as "eyes," or "face," and would apply it extensively throughout the test. Here, the patient is likely neutralizing the anxiety associated with the test and with allowing one's fantasy and affect full reign.

Tight Control or Drowning in Details.   The average number of responses most people give to the Rorschach range between 17 and 27 (Exner 1974). In the obsessive-compulsive patients, two-thirds of the patients either gave less than 15 or more than 30 responses on the Rorschach test. The brief responders either gave terse neutral responses or few but extended emotionally ladened responses. On the other hand, the patients who gave the largest number of responses (40 or more) generally displayed the most primary process as well as more neutralization through language.

Structural Characteristics of the Obsessive Compulsive Patient

Thus far we have seen that obsessive compulsives are marked by the extent to which primitive material has invaded their consciousness and the equally powerful neutralizing strategies these patients have developed to handle these impulses. Unlike the neurotic where the primitive drives never fully reach consciousness except in symbolic or symptomatic forms, and unlike the psychotic where primary process is conscious but defenses have completely failed, most of these obsessive-compulsive patients represent a third possibility where primitive impulse material is conscious and the defenses, other than repression and denial, have not failed. Rather, the defenses that do work are those that neutralize and contain the primary process material. Thus, the central characteristic of most of these patients is this highly charged impasse, a deadlock between the failure of repression and denial, and the success of the neutralizing strategies discussed above and other "containing" defenses such as preoccupation with detail.

In this section of the chapter, I would like to use the formal Rorschach scores more than content to explore further the inability of these patients to modulate the explicit imagery associated with their primitive impulses, and on their inability to release the underlying impulse effectively.

First, let us examine the failure to repress affect-laden imagery. Consider the following response. "Could be modern dancers, dancing on stage. The red things would be part of decorations hanging from the ceiling. Of course, they (the red things) could be blood. They could be shot." The failure to censor the aggression that emerges spoils an otherwise "popular," easily seen response to card III. On the Rorschach, affective responsivity to the environment has frequently been shown to be related to the amount and kind of color used on the Rorschach (Cerbus and Nichols 1963; Exner 1974). At the nonemotive end of the continuum is the "pure form" response that represents factual, nonemotive ego functioning, while at the other extreme is the "pure color" response which represents emotionality undisciplined by rational objectivity. A remarkable number of these patients used this relatively unmodulated color. In the above response, it was blood "because it is red." Moreover, some of these patients also use color in a symbolic, idiosyncratic way. "The red is how our country is split. The outside red represents foreign trouble gnawing away at us. The inside red is our inner troubles" (card X). What is unusual about many of these color-dominated responses is that they often contained "pure form" objects within them. Thus they maintain a mixture of both unrestrained affective images and rational control within the same response.

A second type of score, the movement response, often reflects these patients' inability to release their powerful impulses effectively. Frequently, the obsessive's projected movement included the extremes of both violence and behavioral passivity. In general, all projected movement is related to an inhibition of muscle movement in the subject (Exner 1974), and increases in muscle potential accompany almost all aggressive content responses on the Rorschach (Steele and Kahn 1969). But obsessive patients often give extremely passive movement responses, which are related to behavioral passivity in real life (Exner 1974). Responses such as "flowers floating in a pond," "looks like feet dangling," "a candle dripping" were given by two-thirds of the patients and reflect a certain inner impotence to release their impulses. One can clearly see this inhibition of aggressive impulse with passive movement in the following response: "Bats. The black part gives you the feeling of something very evil. It looks like the bat is sleeping."

The Rorschach protocols seem to suggest two styles of responding among obsessives: some patients appear more preoccupied with the impulse, others with defense. Let us first look at the seven patients who were more preoccupied with the impulse that was unrestrained in their imaginations yet blocked in external expression. This led to a certain diffusion of affect and a personalization of the responses. This diffusion of affect often appeared quite hysterical in style: "Right away I'm caught by all the different colors; I think they're bright," "gives me a feeling of water, movement, splashing," "surging look, like its coming at you very fast," "looks like ice they're climbing, something made of ice, makes me feel cold." These emotive responses seem unanchored in particular forms on the card, were not well controlled by the ego, and reflected a lack of differentiation between the person and his object world. Nevertheless, these patients attempted to control this diffused affective responding by becoming preoccupied with the details of the blot. For the whole group, the average percentage of responses to unusual details on the blot was 16 percent contrasted to 5 percent among normals (Exner 1974).

On the other hand, the better-defended patients ($N = 8$ in our sample) prevented the personalization of the blots mentioned above by distancing themselves, by taking perspective, by assuming a spectator role. This is seen on the Rorschach by giving responses that mention or imply a perspective. Seventy-five percent of these patients gave these vista responses versus 43 percent among the more impulse-oriented patients. A second indication was an emphasis on "looking" responses and "eyes." Sixty percent of the patients gave these; one patient had 24 such responses.

These two subgroups of obsessive-compulsive patients also differed on another dimension, namely, maintaining stable, well-differentiated ego boundaries. On the Rorschach, this failure to maintain adequate ego boundaries can best be measured by penetration responses (Fisher and Cleveland 1958; Goldfried et al. 1971), which are responses that have broken boundaries. Overall, the obsessive patients had a mean of 3.6 penetration responses versus an expected mean of 2.0 (Goldfried et al. 1971). However, the more impulse oriented patients gave 6.9, while the better defended patients gave only 0.9. The most common form of penetration responses was anatomy, which is often interpreted as a reflection of hostility (Phillips and Smith 1953). The average number of anatomy responses given by the total group was 2.4; the more impulse oriented patients gave 3.6; the better defended patients gave none. This compares with an expected of 0.6 among normals (Exner 1974). Examples include "organ from one's body, as if someone opened it up or spread it out," "something being pulled open, stretched out, pinned down, disemboweled and spread out to dry." On the other hand, twice the percentage of responses among the better defended patients (14 percent versus 7 percent from the impulse ridden patients) contained images emphasizing rigid ego boundaries, such as ecto-skeletal animals. For example, one patient said, "These figures remind me of crabs."

Table 1 Obsessive-Compulsive Disorder Patients and the Sensation Seeking Scale

	General Scale	Thrill and Adventure	Experience Seeking	Disinhibition	Boredom Susceptibility
Total	5.8 ± 3.6 (3)	5.8 ± 3.4 (6)	4.8 ± 4.3 (16)	4.7 ± 3.4 (45)	3.4 ± 2.5 (8)
Male	3.9 ± 3.1 (0.5)	4.1 ± 3.0 (0.4)	3.2 ± 2.4 (4)	4.1 ± 3.4 (22)	3.4 ± 2.5 8
Female	8.7 ± 2.7 (11)	8.3 ± 2.2 (28)	7.2 ± 5.4 (25)	5.5 ± 3.5 (65)	...

Note. Data are means ± SD (percentile rank).

However, his next response was a penetration, "The red would be some sort of rib cage."

In summary, the formally scored responses in this section reveal the core conflict of the obsessive-compulsive disorder patient; namely, the impasse between strong primitive impulses and inhibited release. Thus, their color responses suggest a peculiar blending in single responses of both unrestrained emotionality and intellectualized control, while movement responses suggest both images of violent action and passivity. Different patients may emphasize one over the other side in this conflict. Some patients' protocols reflect more of the impulse experiencing side; and their responses suggest diffuse affect, personalization of the material and loose ego boundaries. Other patients appear locked into a more defensive posture, and their protocols reflect a rigid observing ego stance with rigid ego boundaries.

Inhibition and the Sensation Seeking Scale

Further evidence of these patients attempts to inhibit any acting out of their impulses can be seen in the results from the Sensation Seeking Scale which are found in Table 1. In general, the subjects scored extremely low on these measures, the mean percentile rank for the whole sample is 16 percent; males are at the 7th percentile, females at the 32nd. These findings suggest that obsessive-compulsive disorder patients do not seek stimulating activity in the environment (Thrill and Adventure), nor in their inner life (Experience Seeking), nor are they averse to or restless with monotonous, invariant situations (Boredom susceptibility). This is precisely the dampening maneuver one would expect for someone overaroused with primary process material. The Disinhibition subscale was the only scale in the average range. It measures the extent that one seeks sensation through social stimulation and drinking, and it correlates highly with hypomanic type traits. The most likely explanation for the middle range scores is that the scale is extremely constricted at the lower "inhibited" end, and thus simply does not discriminate well in these ranges.

IMPLICATIONS FOR THEORY AND THERAPY

The Rorschach data appear to confirm the observations of Freud, Rado, and other analytic theorists that hostile, sadistic impulses are a central component of this disorder. They are also in accord with a self-report descriptive study by Rachman and DeSilva (1978) of the obsessions of patients and normals. Seventy percent of the obsessions in their sample focused on violence and physical aggression, 17 percent on deviant sexual impulses, another 9 percent on being out of control, and only 4 percent on neutral rote phrases. Obsessions among normals were distributed in approximately the same way, only less vivid, intense, frequent, unacceptable, and discomforting. However, the descriptive Rorschach material also suggests that repression and denial are not very effective at preventing primary process material from becoming conscious. So in contradiction to some Freudian theorists, there is no evidence in this material that there are "even more horrible" unconscious underlying impulses.

If this is the case, then the psychotherapeutic response may better focus on what is present than what might be underlying it. This would entail working with the secondary features of the disorder—the anxiety, rituals, and so forth, as the behaviorists have suggested, as well as helping the patients to accept and deal with the heightened impulses they experience.

The acceptance of aggressive and perhaps sexual impulses and fantasies as a central factor in obsessive-compulsive disorder also may help focus biological explorations. For instance, we know that heightened dysphoric feelings are often associated with behavioral inhibition in humans (e.g., withdrawal in depression, avoidance in anxiety and phobias), whereas pleasurable affect is often related to uninhibited action, as in manic behavior or mild alcoholic intoxication. The relationship of aggression and inhibition may well be another example of this.

While we do not yet understand the neurochemistry of brain functioning well enough to create or test adequately the biological substrate for obsessive-compulsive disorder, we do have some intriguing leads. For example, we do know that low blood platelet monoamine oxidase activity (and therefore perhaps higher monoamine transmitter activity) is correlated with pleasurable affect and uninhibited action in humans (Zuckerman et al. 1980), and that high monoamine oxidase activity may be related to dysphoric affect and decreased social activity (Murphy et al. 1982). There is also a variety of studies with rats relating biogenic amines (dopamine, norepinephrine, and serotonin) to aggression (Barr et al. 1976; File 1975; Welch et al. 1974), general behavioral inhibition (Crow 1977; Ellison 1979), and reduction of activity in novel situations (Ellison 1977). Moreover, the more promising pharmacological agents with obsessive-compulsive patients also implicate these neurotransmitters. However, three important points need to be made. First, if one or more monoamine transmitters are related to aggressive impulses and behavioral inhibition, these systems are probably but a small segment of a larger network, perhaps including both hormonal variables such as testosterone (Dixon 1980; Elias 1981) and the endogenous opiates. Second, none of the rat or human studies cited above suggest that aggressive impulses or behavior, however intense, are caused by abnormal or dysfunctional monoamine transmitter systems, even though pharmacological modifications of them are associated with some changes in behavior. Third, even if we could change the strength of the underlying aggressive impulse, that would probably not make much observable difference in the obsessive-compulsive's general life style. Cognitive and behavioral defenses are very overlearned habits and probably would persist even with their original purpose and motivation removed. Gordon Allport labeled this the "functional autonomy" of habits, and it is the essence of dynamic psychopathology that childhood-established defenses and styles continue beyond the trauma that initiated them. Thus, pharmacologically defusing the aggressive impulse might allow the psychotherapeutic intervention to proceed more rapidly and successfully.

SUMMARY

To summarize, these obsessive-compulsive disorder patients are similar to persons with schizophrenia and mania in that they display an availability of primary process to consciousness, yet are also similar to the compulsive personality disorder in their ability to neutralize and contain this affective material and in their relatively accurate grasp of reality. The very success and power of both the primitive affect to be present in consciousness and of the defensive strategies to control and neutralize it result in an acutely painful impasse, an intensely motivated intransigence and immobility, and ultimately in a devastating debilitation, where active engagement in the world becomes impossible.

References

Barr GA, Gibbons JL, Bridger WH: Neuropharmacology regulation of mouse killing by rats. Behavioral Biology 17:143–159, 1976

Cerbus D, Nichols R: Personality variables and response to color. Psychol Bull 60:566–575, 1963

Crow TJ: Neurotransmitter-related pathways: the structure and function of central monoamine neurons, in Biochemical Correlates of Brain Structure and Function. Edited by Davison AN. New York, Academic Press, 1977

Dixon AF: Androgen and aggressive behavior in primates: a review. Aggressive Behavior 6:37–68, 1980

Elias M: Serum Cortisol, testosterone, and testosterone-binding globulin responses to competitive fighting in human males. Aggressive Behavior 7:215–224, 1981

Ellison GD: Animal models of psychopathology: the low-norepinephrine and low-serotonin rat. Am Psychol 32:1036–1045, 1977

Ellison GD: Animal models of psychopathology: Studies in naturalistic colony environments, in Psychopathology in Animals. Edited by Keegan JD. New York, Academic Press, 1979

Exner JE: The Rorschach: A Comprehensive System. New York, Wiley, 1974

File SE: Effects of parachlorophenylalanine and amphetamine on habituation of orienting. Pharmacol Biochem Behav 3:979–983, 1975

Fisher S, Cleveland SE: Body Image and Personality. Princeton, Van Nostrand, 1958

Goldfried MR, Stricker G, Weiner IB: Rorschach Handbook of Clinical and Research Applications. Englewood Cliffs, NJ, Prentice-Hall, 1971

Holt RR: Manual for the Scoring of Primary Process Manifestations in Rorschach Responses, 10th ed. New York, Research Center for Mental Health of New York University, 1970

Murphy DL, Coursey RD, Haenel T, et al: Platelet monoamine oxidase as a biological marker in the affective disorders and alcoholism, in Biological Markers in Psychiatry and Neurology. Edited by Usdin E, Handin I. New York, Pergamon Press, 1982

Phillips L, Smith JG: Rorschach Interpretation: Advanced Technique. New York, Grune & Stratton, 1953

Rachman S, DeSilva P: Abnormal and normal obsessions. Behav Res Ther 16:233–248, 1978

Salzman L, Thaler FH: Obsessive-compulsive disorders: a review of the literature. Am J Psychiatry 138:286–296, 1981

Schafer R: The Clinical Application of Psychological Tests. New York, International Universities Press, 1948

Schafer R: Psychoanalytic Interpretation in Rorschach Testing. New York, Grune & Stratton, 1954

Steele NM, Kahn MW: Kinesthesis and the Rorschach M response. Journal of Projective Techniques for Personality Assessment 33:5–10, 1969

Welch BL, Hendley ED, Turek I: Norepinephrine uptake into cerebral cortical synaptosomes after one fight or electroconvulsive shock. Science 183:220–221, 1974

Zuckerman M: Sensation Seeking: Beyond the Optimal Level of Arousal. Hillsdale, NJ, Erlbaum, 1979

Zuckerman M, Buchsbaum MS, Murphy DL: Sensation seeking and its biological correlates. Psychol Bull 88:187–214, 1980